If mysticism is but another facet of creativity, then it may be set in motion by some singularly significant incident, such as when one sees a ghost, an elf, or an angel. This first encounter usually triggers one's awareness of much greater reality than once thought.

And it is at the time of that initial contact with the unknown that the new mystic first understands that the artificial concepts to which we have given the designation of sciences are no truer, no more real, than our dreams, visions, and inspirations—all of which have their most profound expression in . . .

OUR SHARED
WORLD OF THE
SUPERNATURAL

OUR SHARED WORLD OF THE SUPERNATURAL

Brad Steiger

A SIGNET VISIONS BOOK

SIGNET
Published by New American Library, a division of
Penguin Putnam Inc., 375 Hudson Street,
New York, New York 10014, U.S.A.
Penguin Books Ltd, 27 Wrights Lane,
London W8 5TZ, England
Penguin Books Australia Ltd, Ringwood,
Victoria, Australia
Penguin Books Canada Ltd, 10 Alcorn Avenue,
Toronto, Ontario, Canada M4V 3B2
Penguin Books (N.Z.) Ltd, 182–190 Wairau Road,
Auckland 10, New Zealand

Penguin Books Ltd, Registered Offices:
Harmondsworth, Middlesex, England

First published by Signet, an imprint of New American Library,
a division of Penguin Putnam Inc.

First Printing, August 2001
10 9 8 7 6 5 4 3 2 1

CONTENTS

OUR SHARED
WORLD OF THE
SUPERNATURAL

1

THE WORLD OF THE
SUPERNATURAL SURROUNDS US

Down through the ages, veritable multitudes of sincere, rational men and women have encountered the supernatural dimension that surrounds and interacts with ordinary three-dimensional reality. Whether their mystical encounters brought them face-to-face with an angel, a ghost, the spirit of a departed loved one, a nature sprite, or a mysterious otherworldly entity, these individuals found themselves touched by the unknown and their lives forever changed.

I may never know the true identity of the being that visited me on that October night in 1940 when I was just a few months away from five years old. Whoever or whatever he was, he opened a passage way to another world, another reality, that for me has never closed. It was this visitation that set me on the path of exploring the unknown, and that has compelled me to embark on a lifelong pursuit of the supernatural.

I was a night person even then. My parents would

put me to bed just after dark, and I would sit on the edge of my bed, looking out the window at the stars and the moon until I would eventually grow sleepy enough to lie back down on my pillow and pull the covers up to my chin. Our old farmhouse was kind of L-shaped, and I was able to look out of my bedroom window and watch my parents through the kitchen window as they sat talking over the day's events at the table.

On this particular night as I sat on my bed looking up at a harvest moon, I heard the sound of someone walking outside on the crisp autumn leaves. For those of you who grew up in towns and cities, it would have been nothing out of the ordinary for you to have heard someone outside the house walking down the street after dark. But when you live on a farm several miles out in the country, it is an occasion of some concern to hear footsteps outside the window—especially after dark when you aren't expecting company.

While I was becoming more than a little anxious about the possibility of an undeclared, unknown person prowling around outside our farmhouse, I was struck by another peculiarity. Bill, our big collie, wasn't making a ruckus. Normally, either friend or stranger would be greeted by persistent yelps of welcome or warning. Where was our faithful, dependable watchdog?

And then I heard a washtub being dragged from the pump at the well. Curiosity and a small sense of alarm caused me to lean closer toward the window glass to investigate.

I jerked back in equal parts of astonishment and fright when I saw a smallish man settling the tub beneath the kitchen window. The light from the kerosene lamp that issued from the window enabled me to see that the peculiar little fellow wore a kind of tapered top hat and was dressed in a one-piece coverall, something like the kind that Dad wore when he worked on machinery. But while Dad's outfit was roomy and bulky, the stranger's coverall was very tight, almost molded to his body.

And then I spotted old Bill. He was crouched by the side of the house, but he wasn't moving or making a sound. It was as if he were somehow transfixed by the very sight of the unexpected visitor.

I thought about opening my window and yelling out, "Sic 'im," to Bill, but I decided against it when I saw that the little man was now standing on the washtub and raising himself on his tiptoes to peer in at my mother and father.

When he got closer to the window, I could see very clearly his large round head, two pointed ears, and the long, slender fingers that grasped the windowsill.

I grew very excited. This was almost as good as seeing Santa Claus. I was certain that I was watching a *nisse*—what we reared in the Scandinavian tradition call a brownie or an elf—during his nocturnal rounds. Perhaps he had come to repair some machinery for Dad or bring in a pail of water for Mom.

I studied him carefully, wanting to memorize just exactly how he looked. He had just a little stub for a nose, and I couldn't really see his eyes all that well until he must have sensed that he, the watcher, was being watched—and he turned to look at me from a distance of no more than seven feet.

Although we were physically separated from one

another by a windowpane, that thin, transparent barrier did nothing to impede the tingle of shock and surprise that I received from those enormous, slanted eyes with their vertical, reptilian or catlike pupils. And the action of his turning his head enabled me to see that what I had at first assumed was a kind of top hat was really a tapered extension of the being's oddly misshapen head.

I felt a sharp jab of fear, and my heart began to thud at my chest. I had a strong sense of knowing that I wasn't supposed to have seen our intruder—whatever he was—and that he was almost as startled and upset as I was—although for obviously very different reasons.

I wanted to scream and to cry out for my parents. For a terrible moment or two, I thought that the little man with the cat's eyes was going to attack me.

But he didn't really seem angry or hostile. It almost appeared as if he were smiling at me.

And the more I looked into the shadowed depths of the being's eyes, the calmer I became. They were already disproportionately large for such a small face, but now they seemed to be expanding even more.

They seemed to grow larger and larger until all I could see were those enchanting eyes.

And then it was morning.

The tin washtub was still against the kitchen wall, but when I went to check on Bill, I was relieved to see that he was already about his morning duties overseeing the pigs and the cattle. The little stranger had apparently left the big collie completely untroubled.

I ran into the kitchen to shatter all possibility of

Mom and Dad having a quiet breakfast. I had exciting news to tell them. A weird little man who looked a lot like an elf, but who had snake or cat eyes and a large elongated head, had spied on them while they had sat talking at the kitchen table.

I received a more complete hearing from my parents regarding my strange encounter than many children of my generation might have been granted. According to Mom, her family claimed a direct relationship to the famous Danish storyteller Hans Christian Anderson. My mother also had vivid gifts for creating imaginative tales, and she had had a number of mystical and eerie experiences in her childhood which had continued into her adult years. Dad's conservative evangelical Lutheranism caused him to exercise more caution toward spiritual dimensions beyond those prescribed by the pulpit of St. Olaf's Church, but he was always quietly tolerant of the beliefs of others.

My parents' individual worldviews provided me with what I believe to have been an excellent balance. I was one of those fortunate children who was allowed to apprehend the world around me on the intuitive and subjective, as well as the material and objective, levels. I have since learned from various psychological studies that have been conducted that those children whose parents occasionally indulge them in fantasy play become adults who are capable of entering trance states, undergoing deeply religious experiences, feeling empathy and compassion for others, and expressing respect for worldviews different from their own. Educators, psychologists, and other observers of our species' behavior patterns have stated that such children also become the adults who are the most flexible in dealing with others.

Although my parents—and especially my mother—delighted in fantasy play, the boundary lines of reality were never blurred. Clear distinctions were drawn early in my childhood between what is real and what is unreal in terms of consensual reality, the material world that we share with others. While my mother was prone to undergo the occasional mystical experience, my father insisted that all alleged supernatural occurrences in our home be subjected to objective analyses. Natural, logical explanations for suspected paranormal phenomena were always to be preferred before anyone pronounced an occurrence as otherworldly.

There was a time when I truly felt that Dad would accept only what he could hold in his own hands and appreciate with his own physical senses. And yet, this serious-minded man exhibited a childlike faith in his spiritual beliefs and a childlike enthusiasm for playing on the town softball team well into his forties. I learned from my parents' example that it is important to be able to become childlike (that's not *childish*) in order to continue to look at reality with fresh vision.

I knew that the strange visitor to our farm on that October night in 1940 was not a creature of my imagination. He was not the by-product of fanciful fantasy play. And whoever he was, he had somehow activated a potent mental mechanism within my psyche. By his very appearance, he had demonstrated to me that we are not alone in the universe.

Today, whenever I recall those large, compelling eyes, I am forced to accept that there exist other intelligences who can manifest in our dimension of reality, who sometimes resemble us, who very often seem curious about us, and who might even care about us in some way. While others may believe that the entity that visited us that long-ago night was an elf, a *nisse*, or—as some have suggested—an extraterrestrial UFOnaut, I prefer to think of him simply as a multidimensional being, my personal proof of "The Other."

Of course, there have been many listeners who have heard my story and suggested that he was nothing more than a vivid character in a child's dream.

If that is true, then he was the central character in the most profound dream of my entire life, one that still compels me to pursue the supernatural sixty years later.

And if my strange visitor appeared only in a little boy's dream, then, amazingly, a little girl was having the same dream on the same long-ago evening in another Iowa village just a few miles away.

A Painting of a Long-Ago Visitor

In July 1987, my wife Sherry and I, together with our friends Patricia Rochelle and Jon Diegel, were attending the Outer Space Art Show of Luis Romero in Sedona, Arizona. I was both pleased and shocked when I suddenly came face-to-face with a painting of one particular alien portrait. Incredibly, I now beheld the nearest facsimile that I had ever seen of the entity of my childhood encounter, and I experienced a very strong sense of déjà vu in my solar plexus.

I knew that Luis had heard the story of my en-

counter at a recent social gathering in his home, so I
made the assumption that my childhood experience
had been the inspiration for this remarkable alien
portrait. "This is the closest that I have ever seen
to the entity that I encountered as a child," I told
the artist.

Luis smiled and said that he thought I would have
such a shock of recognition when I saw the work,
but he went on to tell me that he had not done the
painting from my descriptions. He had painted the
entity according to the specifications of a woman
who had had a similar encounter with such a being
as a child and who had continued to interact with
her visitor from another world.

Luis had no sooner informed me of the source for
his painting when the lady under discussion walked
into the art show. Her name was Sharon Reed, and
to my astonishment, she had spent a portion of her
childhood in West Bend, Iowa. Bode, where we have
our family farm, and West Bend are neighboring
small towns. Even though we had never met each
other while growing up, Sharon and I obviously had
a fascinating acquaintance in common.

As we talked and compared our recollection of the
visitor, we discovered that the details of our encounter with the eavesdropping "visitor" were nearly
identical; and while we cannot prove that our visitations occurred on exactly the same night, it had to
have been at least within a few days of each other's
experience.

Contact with the entity had changed Sharon's life
as it had changed mine. Our universe had been
opened wide when we were only children, and such
an expansion of the perimeters of reality had permit-

ted us to continue to explore the far reaches of the unknown as adults.

The Individual Mystical Experience Opens a Door to the Unknown

In the sixty years since my childhood encounter with the mysterious entity, I have met thousands of men and women who have experienced an interaction with supernatural beings that appeared to them as spirits, angels, elves, holy figures, or extraterrestrial visitors. These people are sincere in their recounting of their experiences and are unshaken by the disbelief or doubts of others.

While in many instances there is little or no physical evidence to demonstrate any kind of proof of the encounter to the skeptical materialist, the individuals who received such unexpected visitations from nonmaterial beings are left with an unyielding conviction that their lives have been forever changed. For some reason which they may never fully understand, they underwent an individual mystical experience with some facet of the supernatural. They were somehow invited to participate in a very personal, very subjective, extremely illuminating experience that is as intimate, as life-altering, as revelatory, as unifying as the human psyche can perceive.

The great philosopher William James once observed that the Mother Sea, the fountainhead of all religions, lies in the mystical experience of the individual. All theologies, all ecclesiastical establishments, he contended, were but secondary growths superimposed.

On January 23, 1994, *USA Today* published the fascinating results of the exhaustive analysis of the most recent comprehensive data available of private spiritual experience based on a national sociological survey conducted for the National Opinion Research Center, University of Chicago, which revealed that more than *two-thirds* of all Americans claim to have had at least one mystical experience. To put that another way, approximately 145 million Americans have been touched by the supernatural.

Of that number:

- 67.3 percent say that they experienced some form of extrasensory perception, such as telepathically communicating with someone who was far away from them.
- 28.3 percent claim an experience with clairvoyance, the ability to see events as they happen at a great distance.
- 39.9 percent are convinced that they have communicated with spirits of the deceased.
- 31.5 percent have experienced a connection to a powerful spiritual force that seemed to elevate their consciousness.

Jeffrey S. Levin, an associate professor at Eastern Virginia Medical School, Norfolk, Virginia, states that such mystical experiences as those reported above have been around "since time immemorial." And while there have been periods of history wherein supernatural experiences were freely accepted and even encouraged, the emphasis on the material sciences in the nineteenth and twentieth centuries have caused people to ignore or rationalize such mystical experiences out of the fear of being regarded as superstitious. Until only recently, Levin observes, "some kind of stigma" may have prevented more people from acknowledging their paranormal encounters.

While only 5 percent of the present population report experiencing such mystical encounters and episodes on a regular basis, Levin states, such occurrences are becoming "more common with each successive generation."

Although the Western world has not really encouraged the individual mystical experience for the past couple of centuries, it is becoming quite clear to many serious-minded theologians, sociologists, philosophers, and other observers of the contemporary scene that all people may be potential mystics, just as there are potential poets, artists, and musicians. If mysticism is but another facet of creativity, then it may be set in motion by some singularly significant activating incident, such as when one glimpses a ghost, an elf, or an angel. The manifestation of this psychic catalyst somehow activates the percipient into receiving his or her first glimpse of a much greater reality that appears to stretch to the farthermost reaches of the universe.

And it is at the time of that initial contact with the unknown that the newly activated mystic first understands that the artificial concepts to which we have given the designation of sciences are no truer, no realer, than our dreams, visions, and inspirations.

When an individual achieves a mystical sense of Oneness with All That Is, he or she truly perceives that the only eternal truths are the immaterial products of our soul, our imagination, and our inspirations—all of which have their most profound expression in our shared world of the supernatural.

I also believe quite strongly that there exists an as yet unidentified form of energy that is the source of all so-called magical or supernatural powers, and I believe that the human psyche serves as a conduit for this force. Throughout history, certain gifted shamans, seers, and prophets have channeled this energy, this "supernatural force," to create apparent miracles of healing, levitation, mind-over-matter, prophecy, and communication with spiritual intelligences on other levels of being.

The World of the Supernatural Has a Varied Cast of Characters

In *Shadow World*, I listed a number of the spirits and multidimensional beings most often associated with haunting phenomena. To summarize briefly, I named such supernatural interlopers as the following:

Spirits of the Dead—Earthbound spirits who have not yet progressed into the Light of a higher spiritual dimension.

Nature Spirits—Whether you term these beings fairies, devas, elves—or any one of dozens of other names for such nature spirits—they are sometimes benevolent, most often mischievous, and occasionally malignant.

Deiform Spirits—Ancient people may have worshipped these entities as gods and goddesses. They seem most often to manifest around old ruins and burial sites and appear frequently as majestic, archetypal, godlike beings.

Spirit Parasites—Quite likely the traditional demons, Spirit Parasites are especially dominant in places where murders or other acts of violence have occurred. They are capable of possessing unaware or vulnerable humans.

Spirit Mimics—Strange "in-between beings" who often pose as ordinary men and women until some peculiar or out-of-place action or response gives them away. Their goals remain difficult to ascertain from our human perspective.

Adding the Beings of Light

And now, in this present book, we must add angels, spirit guides, spirit teachers, and Light Beings to those entities who may visit us from the world of the supernatural. But we must also point out that different people may be speaking of very different otherworldly beings when they speak of angelic or spirit guardians. In many instances the name one gives to those benevolent supernatural beings who concern themselves with the activities of mortal humans is largely a matter of semantics or of one's prior religious-cultural background.

For example, a heavenly angel to one percipient may well be termed a spirit guide by another. "Angel" most often has religious connotations. "Spirit guide" does not. To someone in the shamanic tradition, the spirit guide may often take the form of a totemic animal, such as a wolf, a bear, or a cougar, and serve as the gatekeeper to the Other Side. To a spiritualist, a spirit guide is the entity who brings spirits of the deceased to communicate with an entranced medium.

And then if we are able to draw distinctions between spirit guides and angels, we may still be left with a difference of opinion when it comes to a clear definition of who or what constitutes an angel. A popular belief has it that when a human being dies, he or she becomes an angel. While I always wish to avoid any kind of rigid dogma when exploring the supernatural, I must point out that the holy books of the great world religions are in agreement that those entities that we call angels are an earlier and separate order of creation from us humans. Therefore, according to these ancient teachings, a human does not die and become an angel.

The Judeo-Christian Bible declares that we mortals were created a "little lower than the angels," and we join the angelic host in the heavenly realm as distinctly human personalities and energy forms. The Qur'an states that there are three distinct species of intelligent beings in the universe. There are first the angels [malak], a high order of beings created of Light; second, the al-jinn, ethereal, perhaps even multidimensional entities; and then humans, fashioned of the stuff of Earth and born into material bodies. Buddhism teaches that there are bodhisattvas, beings who have earned Nirvana but who stay behind to help suffering humanity. And each of the beings thus described in the holy books may be somehow involved in the lives of those of us material beings who are connected to them by means of our nonmaterial souls.

As you will soon perceive in the pages of this book, the world of the supernatural is rich in yielding exciting and enriching mystical experiences with a host of fascinating spiritual beings. As you will discover by reading the true, personal experiences of the men and women who have shared their otherworldly encounters for this book, the inhabitants of the vast supernatural domain can express themselves in a seemingly endless variety of guises—as beautiful, caring, compassionate angelic guides; as mysterious, ghostly visitors from another place in time; as Light Beings who come to bring miracle healings; or as hostile apparitions intent on driving out all living inhabitants from their earthly domiciles.

You may deem some of these accounts provocative, a few a bit frightening, and many others truly inspirational and uplifting—but each one of them offers profound evidence of the supernatural dominion that surrounds our ordinary three-dimensional material world.

2

LIVING WITH THE MANY GHOSTS OF INSPIRATION HOUSE

The world of the supernatural can reach out at any time and envelop any one of us. It matters not who it has singled out to summon across its borders, for the supernatural is no respecter of persons. Whether we be rich or poor, college educated or street-smart, common laborer or white-collar professional, we are all pilgrim souls in an uncharted land when we journey into the dimensions of the unknown.

In late September 1984, Rita Gallagher, a popular romance novelist, moved into an old Victorian mansion in the small central Texas town of Navasota. In her eyes, the house was the perfect writer's retreat, for in addition to being the author of such novels as *Passion Star*, *Shadows on the Wind*, and *Shadowed Destiny*, Rita was a highly respected teacher of writing. She knew that her students would love the rambling old mansion, so she leased the house with an option to buy.

No one at the real estate agency bothered to tell her that the house hadn't been lived in for more than ten years—or that it was haunted.

Her first night in the old mansion explained why the lease price had been so reasonable. Shortly after 3:00 A.M., there came a rustling sound in the back hall. Then Rita heard slow footsteps, with one foot dragging, making their way from the front hall between the bedrooms and descending the main staircase.

Though Rita peered up and down the corridor—and even ventured out to the banister—she saw nothing. There were only the sounds of an invisible presence descending the broad staircase.

And then suddenly she was looking into the sad eyes of a young man with shaving cream on his face—who then promptly disappeared.

Recalling the startling occurrence, Rita said, "I wouldn't have been afraid if he had stayed and talked with me. But his sudden appearance and disappearance made my first night in the house a terrifying one."

When morning came, Rita tested the steps. "The third one down was a creaking one. A board on the top landing had a different sound, and the fourth step above the lower landing creaked more loudly than the others."

On the next evening, shortly after 3:00 A.M. when the creaking sounds came again, Rita was able to determine the location of the ghost's descent to the main floor.

"The ghostly walk ended in the kitchen," she said. "Until dawn purpled the sky, the sound of rattling pots, pans, and dishes echoed faintly throughout the house. Then the ghost made the trip back upstairs and, with a rustling sound, vanished into the back hall."

Ghost or no ghost, Rita could not afford to lose her investment.

And she had a book to write.

She decided to work around the ghost and live out the lease.

The next day, she tried to hire a maid and was informed in no uncertain tones that there wasn't a maid in town who would even enter the house, much less work in it.

Learning to Live with a Schedule Established by Noisy Ghosts

Rita recalls that she slept very little in the next two weeks. Then she realized that the ghost's pattern never really changed and that it never walked until shortly after 3:00 A.M.

"And it never entered my room," she said. "I could sleep until that time each night without disturbance."

The Westminster chimes of the clock in the entrance hall tolled the quarter hour, half hour, and hour—until deep night. But then, Rita had observed, "From 3:00 A.M. until dawn streaked the skies, the chimes were strangely muffled, gurgling, almost as though they were ringing through water."

It was Rita's habit to leave her bedroom door open and the newel post lamp at the foot of the main staircase burning all night. Light filtered up the open stairwell to the cathedral ceiling on the second floor.

Shadows of banisters on three sides of the stairwell stretched across the wide hall. Though dim, there was always enough light to see anyone—or *any-thing*—passing through the corridor.

Rita automatically awakened shortly before the spectral rustling sounds began, and she stayed out of the halls after 3:00 A.M.

With clockwork regularity, after 3:00 A.M. the halls were given over to the ghost. And then, one night, Rita discovered that she had to make that plural. Other footsteps, separate and distinctive from the fa-miliar ghostly tread, had manifested. Now, after the rustling sounds, the footsteps of what seemed to be an elderly woman wandered the hall, descended the main staircase, and walked back to the kitchen.

According to Rita:

Sometimes after she [the female ghost] reached the kitchen, the rest of the house was silent. Other times, it seemed, her walk evoked further manifestations. Now and then I heard an intermittent, murmuring conversation be-tween a man and a woman, just low enough that words were indiscernible. Every so often a woman's heartrending sob lasted barely a full second.

Occasionally there were knockings and heavy sighs, and once in a while there came the tinkle of glasses, faint piano music, and laughter. Shortly before dawn I was frequently awakened by the sound of something heavy being dragged over the third floor above my room.

Gaining a Canine Companion to Guard Her

In mid-October, Rita went to Beaumont, Texas, for the Golden Triangle Writers' Guild Annual Conference. On the way she planned to visit a friend, a fellow writer who lived in San Antonio.

"When I arrived, I found my friend in tears," Rita said. "Jupiter, her beloved German shepherd, had inexplicably changed from a good-natured, obedient pet to an angry, unpredictable behemoth. He had bitten neighbors, friends, meter men, and the postman. Just a week before I arrived, he had broken free of their home by chewing up the back doorframe. Then he proceeded to dig up the roses in the neighbors' yard and run down the street knocking over garbage cans, threatening anyone who came near him. Jupiter's record at the county dog pound convinced the authorities that he was a dog gone bad, and my friend's husband had promised that he would put the shepherd down while she was at the writers' conference."

Rita loves dogs. It had been less than a year since her beloved cockapoo, Cleopatra, had died of old age. She had never met Jupiter, but she knew that he had registration papers that recorded nine champions in his bloodline. She also knew that the first four years of his life had passed without incident.

"I felt a strong compulsion to save Jupiter," she said. "I told my friend and her husband that since I lived two hundred miles from San Antonio, I would take him far away from the place where he had got into so much trouble."

After giving her firm warning about Jupiter's vicious nature, the couple agreed to Rita's proposition; and when the conference in Beaumont was over, she drove back to San Antonio to pick up the German shepherd.

"I must admit that the mere size of the magnificent animal was intimidating," Rita said. "He had a great, leonine head and a regal bearing. He studied me through intelligent, golden eyes, and I stared back at him. It was love at first sight. He walked across the room and placed his giant head in my lap. We were meant for each other."

Rita experienced no problems with Jupiter on the long drive from San Antonio to Navasota. It was three in the afternoon when they arrived at Rita's haunted house.

Jupiter Meets the Many Ghosts of the Old Texas Mansion

"Jupiter walked into the enormous hall, and I followed him through the loftily ceilinged parlor into the chandeliered dining room, and across the main hall into the library," Rita remembered. "When we entered the back hall, he paused a moment at the foot of the steep servants' staircase. Staring upward, he sniffed, raised his head abruptly, and whined."

As Jupiter ascended the servants' staircase to the second floor, Rita was right behind him. Then, as the big German shepherd continued up the narrow steps to the third floor, she waited below.

"Just before reaching the opening landing, Jupiter stiffened, and his ruff came up like a lion's mane," Rita said. "With an earsplitting howl, he backed swiftly downstairs and, staring intently upward, sat down and pressed against me.''

Rita saw nothing, but she *felt* the same presence that she had noted on her first night in the old mansion.

At the immediate foot of the stairs there was a small room that Rita—for no reason she knew then—called the nursery. Jupiter wasn't moving. He sat firmly at Rita's feet, alternately cocking his head, staring, and whining.

Deciding to test him further, Rita opened the door to the nursery.

Curious, Jupiter poked his head into the room. Then, turning quickly, he threw himself against Rita and literally pushed her from the back of the house into the main hall.

Woman and dog walked together down the wide corridor between spacious bedrooms. Side by side they descended the broad, sweeping staircase into the main entrance hall. Stained glass bordered a wavy window that ended barely an inch above the lower landing, and with a sigh, Jupiter settled down there.

"He had found his place," Rita said. "For the rest of our time in that house, he spent his days gazing at the passing scene. That night, and every night thereafter, he slept on a rug beside the bed in my large second-floor room.''

Jupiter's first night in the house was an uneasy one, and he moved restlessly on his rug beside Rita's bed. As Rita recalled Jupiter's initiation into the ghostly company in the old Texas mansion:

When the old lady began walking, Jupiter leaped to his feet, nails clicking, and walked across the polished floor to stop just inside the doorway. Cocking his head, he looked out at the dimly lighted hall, first one way, then the other.

The footsteps came closer. As they passed my bedroom door, Jupiter's ruff stood straight up. Then, front legs moving like pistons, he slid backward on his rump over the floor to his rug, where he put his paws over his eyes and gave a low whine.

When the ghost of the elderly woman walked on Jupiter's second night in the mansion, he left his rug and went to the foot of Rita's bed. As the eerie sounds disappeared into the rooms below, he went back to his rug, put his paws over his eyes, and whimpered.

On the third night when the spectral footsteps passed their door, Jupiter merely raised his head, then went back to sleep. "It was as if he were saying, 'Oh, the hell with it,' " Rita observed.

Jupiter Becomes the Official Protector of Guests in Inspiration House

Two months after Jupiter's arrival, Patricia, one of Rita's students who was going through a divorce, came to live with them in the mansion that had now been christened Inspiration House.

"Jupiter was our protector," Rita said. "He would investigate each new manifestation as it occurred.

Then, apparently realizing that there was nothing he could do about it, he made no further effort when it occurred again. He just accepted the phenomena, as we all learned to do."

But daylight or darkness, Jupiter was always alert. "Whether alone or together, when my students or I would walk the halls or go upstairs, Jupiter appeared beside us," Rita recalled. "Now and then he would suddenly step in front and gently, but firmly, push us in the other direction."

Over time, Rita had become convinced that there was nothing to fear from the ghosts that walked Inspiration House. Except for her encounter with the young man with the shaving cream on his face during her first evening in the old mansion, none of the other entities had ever been seen.

Although the auditory manifestations were obvious as they moved about the mansion, Rita observed that "for the most part, they seemed to be on a never-ending soundtrack, each entity performing intermittently. There seemed to be nothing threatening at all in the old house."

But one late summer afternoon, Rita discovered that she had been wrong. Something menacing did exist in the old mansion.

Among the Friendly Ghosts, a Menacing Presence Manifests

The house had been completely "ghost-free" during the daylight hours ever since Rita moved in, but on this particular afternoon, while she ran errands, Patricia was terrified to hear the sound of heavy footsteps thudding up the back servants' staircase. She had been seated in the seminar room, evaluating manuscripts, when the disturbances began; and even though Jupiter lay at her feet, she was badly frightened by the manifestation.

With a low, deep, warning growl, the big German shepherd chased after the unseen intruder. Summoning her own courage, Patricia followed Jupiter until the footsteps suddenly ceased in the middle of the main hallway on the second floor.

Jupiter whimpered and sat down abruptly. His invisible quarry had vanished, leaving him puzzled and confused.

In the days that followed, the heavy footsteps sounded spasmodically through the halls. But Jupiter chose not to give further pursuit of the invisible intruder. He would only whine and nestle close to Rita's feet.

One afternoon, with Jupiter beside her as usual, Rita was seated with Patricia and the bookkeeper in the large room that they had established as an office. While Patricia marked manuscripts and the bookkeeper made ledger entries, Rita busily edited the last chapter of her book.

Then, all at once, Rita felt as though she were engulfed in a pillar of ice:

It was hard to catch my breath, and my heart felt like a large, heavy rock in my chest. I could neither move nor speak. Patricia went on writing; the bookkeeper went on working; and I was terrified!

But Jupiter, snarling menacingly, scrambled to his feet. Ruff standing straight up around his neck, he sank his teeth into my heavy slacks and literally pulled me from the chair toward the door.

As soon as I was pulled from the icy pillar, I could breathe again. But the pain in my chest lasted into the next day. It took even longer to get rid of the chill. It was then that I realized that *something* in the house was far from benign.

Two days later, while Rita was writing upstairs with Jupiter at her feet, the bookkeeper was the one who became enveloped in the deadly chill. This time, however, it was Patricia who pulled the woman free from the icy spell.

"Ministers, priests, and psychic investigators who came to Inspiration House all confirmed what we had already determined," Rita said. "There were multiple hauntings in the old mansion. There was the old woman, the young man, a younger woman, a child, and the heavy man whose footsteps sounded intermittently throughout our afternoons.

"And then there was the threatening, chilling entity that seemed determined to snuff out my life and that of my bookkeeper."

More than a thousand writers and others associated with the publishing world visited Inspiration House during the two and a half years that Rita and Jupiter shared their turf with eerie interlopers from the spirit world. In spite of the rumors about Inspiration House being haunted, student writers, editors, and literary agents came there to participate in various writing programs sponsored by Rita Gallagher.

"Some students left after the first night and thereafter only came for daytime tutoring," Rita said.

"Others, traveling from greater distances, stayed at a nearby motel."

Rita always told newly arriving guests that bathroom privileges were cut off between 3:00 A.M. and dawn. "Some laughed. Others accepted the edict without question."

Jupiter became not only Rita's guardian and that of her secretary, but the protector of all who came to Inspiration House. After dark, without being summoned, he would escort each guest through the upstairs hall to the bathroom. Then, after waiting outside the door, he conducted them back to their beds.

Rita remembered that she often heard Patricia cry herself out of a nightmare in her room across the hall. Her own dreams were also often strange and frightening.

"I would be brought out of a fearful, surrealistic dream by Jupiter's tongue licking my face," Rita said.

Enduring a "Dreadful" Two Weeks Before Leaving the Old Mansion

Having at last completed her book, Rita realized how much energy it had taken just to live in the haunted mansion. Jupiter had lost a great deal of weight. He slept little, and now and then appeared to be tormented by something unseen. Although the veterinarian said that Jupiter's health was good, Rita knew that he was suffering.

The novel was finished. Patricia's divorce was finalized. They decided to move from the old house.

"Our last two weeks in the mansion were dread-ful," Rita said.

Old-fashioned push-button light switches were turned rapidly off and on. Water ran intermit-tently. Toilets were flushed. Doors slammed.

In broad daylight, books were lifted from their shelves, hoisted two or three feet in the air, then dropped to the floor.

Sometimes Patricia's frantic voice called to me. With Jupiter beside me, I would run up-stairs only to discover that she had been in the kitchen or the downstairs bathroom and hadn't called me at all. Other times, it was my voice that Patricia heard calling her.

Two or three times in those final fearful days in Inspiration House, Jupiter was beset by unseen entities.

"At nine or ten at night, with Patricia in her bed reading and me in mine watching television, Jupiter would lie in the hall between our rooms," Rita said. "Suddenly, ruff high around his neck, he would howl, then scramble to the other end of the hall, where, trembling, he cowered in the corner.

"When we went to him, petting him and speaking soothing words, his golden eyes were wide, staring beyond us at something we could not see.

"Then the torture would continue, and the poor dog would scramble to the other end of the upper hall."

The Spirit of a Dear Friend Visits the New Inspiration House

In late March 1987, Rita, Patricia, and Jupiter moved to Conroe, Texas. This time, instead of an old, haunted Victorian mansion, the new Inspiration House was a modern fifteen-room home with maids' quarters, wide lawns, trees—and no ghosts!

During their stay in the new Inspiration House, Rita recalled only one ghostly incident. Shortly before Thanksgiving, their attorney, who was also a member of their Board of Directors for Inspiration House and a dear friend, died suddenly. Along with Patricia's mother, she and Patricia attended the funeral.

That evening grew cold, rare for southeast Texas. With a roaring fire in the fireplace and with Jupiter lying on the stone hearth, the three women grew nostalgic.

"Staring into the flames, we spoke of our deceased friend," Rita said. "We discussed her love of animals in general and of Jupiter in particular. We spoke of her love of roses and good books. We relived the great times that we had had together. We all loved her. And Jupiter loved her too."

Rita and her late friend had often discussed the question of life after death and promised each other that, if at all possible, whoever passed over first would give some sign to those dear ones left behind.

"Suddenly Jupiter jumped up and ran to the sliding glass doors that opened onto the deck," Rita said. "It was early for his nightly walk, but grabbing a sweater, I opened the doors and followed him outside."

It was an established part of Jupiter's nightly routine to bound down the steps to the garden below. This time, however, with wagging tail, he went to the head of the stairs and stopped.

"Bobbing his head, he emitted glad little cries, exactly as he did when greeting a friend," Rita said. "Puzzled, I leaned against the railing and watched.

"Then I was overwhelmed by the strong aroma of *roses!* I was literally *enveloped* in roses. My nostrils were filled with them, and it seemed as though my skin were being caressed with their soft velvety touch."

With his tail still wagging, Jupiter bounded joyfully toward the stairs again and halted abruptly. Then, whining, tail between his legs, he rejoined Rita.

When they entered the house, Rita informed the others what had occurred. They expressed regret that she hadn't called them to experience the perfume of the spirit roses. They had tea and continued talking about their deceased friend.

"Less than an hour later, Jupiter jumped up, wagged his tail, and scampered about, making joyful, growly noises in his throat," Rita said. "And all the while *the scent of roses filled the room.* When the aroma faded, Jupiter ceased his happy scampering as abruptly as he had begun. Then, head down, he resumed his position on the hearth. This time we *all* knew that our friend had given us a sign."

In August 1988, Jupiter became ill with cancer, and after two months of medication and the opinions of several veterinarians, the sorrowful decision had to be made to end the great German shepherd's terrible suffering.

"On our last night together, he lay on his rug beside my bed while I spoke softly to him," Rita said.

"I thanked him for all he had done to make my life happier. I told him that I loved him, and his eyes told me that he loved me, too."

Rita is convinced that on some level of awareness, Jupiter had known that it was his destiny to intertwine his life with Rita's and that it was his job to protect her from harm, his fated duty to guard her from those unseen presences in the old Texas mansion.

"And he did that beautifully," Rita said. "During his four years with me, Jupiter protected me from both seen and unseen predators. He knew my every thought, my every mood, my every fear. And always, *always*, he was there, guarding, guiding, and—most of all—loving those in his care."

3

LUCY FRITCH, THE FRIENDLY SPIRIT

In the 1960s, Sandra and Russell Moore built a very successful photography business in Mississippi by traveling to such outlets as Sears and Kmart and offering low-priced photographs to their customers.

"The stores loved us, because their sales soared when people explored the merchandise and made purchases while waiting to have their pictures taken," Sandra said. "Then, three weeks later when the customers returned to look at their proofs and order their pictures, store sales rose again."

The Moores' traveling photography business soon expanded and prospered until it grew to include twenty-three photographers, a staff of sales personnel, and their own photo-finishing plant.

Then, in 1963, they decided to open a studio as well, a splendid "House of Photography" in a stately old Vicksburg Colonial mansion that they would remodel and modernize. That was when they made the acquaintance of Lucy Fritch, the friendly ghost.

Sandra said that the three-story house was very much in need of repair: "It required wiring for electricity in each of its fourteen very large rooms. The wallboards were very rough and very wide—twelve-inch boards—and covered with plaster, clay, and old 1800s newspapers. Most of the rooms had been wallpapered with a velveteen finish. The attic had windows, but had never really been finished as a third floor. The mansion had a basement that was as large as the main structure, but it had never been finished."

The Moores decided that the six large rooms on the first floor would be their photography studio, show room, display room, and card shop. They knew that they had their work cut out for them, for in each room the ceilings were fourteen feet high with large ceiling decorations and elaborate chandeliers. The hardwood floors had been installed with wooden pegs, rather than nails, and each room had a floor-to-ceiling fireplace. There was also an abundance of windows in the rooms, each elaborate portal extending from about two feet off the floor to the ceiling.

A winding staircase led to the second floor, which was laid out in much the same pattern as the lower floor with the exception of a long hallway that led to a balcony with elaborate rails and banisters. The Moores declared this floor with its five bedrooms to be their living area and built new bathrooms and a kitchen to accommodate a comfortable lifestyle.

Sandra and Russell worked on their remodeling project for nearly two years, converting the old 1800s mansion to modern living while, at the same time, respecting the era in which it had been constructed.

"Interestingly," Sandra observed, "there was another old mansion exactly like ours built next door, only about twenty feet apart. There were only these two houses on that block, and the backyards were adjacent to one another. Immediately behind us were the Civil War headquarters of General Pemberton and the old horse stables were still there on all three properties."

Something Kept Opening the Bedroom Door

Sandra said that they had noticed "strange things" happening around them while they were in the process of remodeling the mansion, but they were just too busy to pay them serious attention.

A steady series of haunting phenomena seemed to begin in earnest on the night when J.R., one of the Moores' traveling photographers from Georgia, was staying over in a second-floor bedroom that had been especially reserved for visiting employees.

"J.R. had retired for the evening when suddenly the door to his room flew open," Sandra recalled. "He got up, checked the hallway, found nothing, closed the door, and went back to bed. Then the door flew open again."

After the door had opened of its own volition the third time, the photographer came to the family room and told the Moores of the strange happenings.

"When we went to the room to investigate," Sandra said, "we immediately smelled gas fumes. J.R. had lowered the jet too far and it was leaking fumes. We put him in another room, and all was well.

Though at that time we couldn't figure out why the door had kept opening and closing."

The Haunting Sounds
of a Baby's Cries

About a week later, around nine o'clock in the evening, while Sandra and Russell and an overnight guest were watching television in the second-floor family room, they heard a baby crying.

Sandra yelled, "Oh, my God! Someone must have accidentally left a baby in the studio!"

The Moores and their guest rushed downstairs and searched all the first-floor rooms.

They found no baby. And nothing that could have made such a plaintive, haunting sound.

"Then, as we started back up the staircase, we heard the baby's crying coming from the basement," Sandra said, recalling the eerie occurrence. "So we rushed down there—and found nothing."

From that night on, the ghostly phenomena seldom abated.

Lights turned on and off in various rooms.

Photography equipment was moved around.

Packs of cigarettes kept appearing in a workroom that was posted off-limits to smokers.

An old French coin materialized on Sandra's vanity.

A radio would begin to play in the downstairs darkroom after everyone had retired for the evening.

"We all accepted the fact that we had a ghost, a spirit, in our old mansion," Sandra said.

A Regular Ghostly Arrival and Mysterious Music

After everyone on the staff had taken notice of one or more ghostly manifestations, Nancy, the Moores' receptionist, told them that every day, at precisely four o'clock, the heavy front entrance door would open. Nancy could not ignore the phenomenon, for the door also bore a bell that would ring when it was opened.

"Nancy said that there would also be a breeze at the same time, as if someone had come in," Sandra said.

It was about that same time that the Moores began hearing classical music in their bedroom at night.

"It was very soft, soothing music," Sandra recalled. "I opened the windows to see if it was coming from next door. I turned on the radio to try to find a station with the same music. I could never determine from where the music originated."

Lucy Fritch Materializes and Introduces Herself

Then one night after they had gone to bed, Sandra was just dozing off when Russell told her to "quit it!"

"We had our backs to each other," Sandra said, "so I had no idea what he was talking about. Then he said it again, 'Quit it!' "

Sandra asked her husband just what it was that she was supposed to stop doing.

"Quit blowing on my neck!" Russell said grumpily. "I'm trying to sleep."

Sandra told him that he was just dreaming, and after a few minutes, she could hear from the sound of his regular breathing that he had fallen asleep.

"I was just nodding off myself," Sandra said, "when I heard a lady's voice say, 'Sandra, Sandra, look at me! I'm Lucy Fritch!' "

Then Sandra saw their ghost. "She was standing at the foot of our canopy bed. She wore a long, flowing gown and a white shawl. In her right hand she held a child's whirligig, and she was blowing into it, making it spin. I sat up—and she vanished."

Sandra woke Russell and told him that she had just seen the ghost that had been heard or felt throughout the old mansion. "And her name is Lucy Fritch," she said, after she had described their ethereal housemate.

"Well, now at least we know what to call her," Russell said. "I guess it was Lucy who was teasing me by blowing on the back of my neck."

Satisfied with an answer to the mystery of their ghost, Russell yawned, rolled over, and went back to sleep.

Sandra remembered being left wide-awake for a long while by Lucy's materialization.

A Lively and Compassionate Spirit

The next day, Sandra called the local museum to inquire if there were any records concerning the mansion in which they resided. She also told the lady who was so courteously answering her questions all about the manifestation of Lucy Fritch.

"Well, she saved that young man's life and just

maybe saved all of you when she led you to discover that gas leak," the woman said matter-of-factly, as if she were quite accustomed to hearing people ask about ghosts in their old houses. From the tone of her voice, Sandra inferred that the lady felt that she and their overnight guest should have been grateful for the spirit's warning. Then she informed Sandra of a young man in Warren County who was a "bit of a ghost hunter," and she said that she would have him get in touch with the Moores.

The "ghost hunter" arrived and began his investigation of the old mansion, and according to Sandra, Lucy manifested daily. "The big front door opened and closed each day at four o'clock when we assumed Lucy took her daily walk," Sandra said. "Lucy continued to play her music—and sometimes she would play some prank on the investigator, and we could hear her laugh. Although the ghost hunter seemed sincere and determined to learn more about the ghost in our home, Lucy's practical jokes proved to be more than he could take—so he abruptly terminated his research."

Sandra bought a large antique cherry wood wardrobe for one of the bathrooms upstairs, and for some unknown reason, Lucy just didn't like it.

"She made lots of noises in that bathroom at night until I had to yell at her, 'Lucy, stop all that racket and let us rest!'

"She would stop slamming the drawers and making a fuss for that night, but the next evening she would be at that wardrobe once again."

Margaret Has a Very Special Friend Help with Her Schoolwork

The Moores' daughter, Margaret, was in fourth grade at that time, and she soon made friends with Lucy. Sometimes Margaret would sit on the floor of her room with flour paste and construct certain projects, such as a map of the United States. After the flour mixture dried, she would paint all the states in different colors.

Margaret told her parents that Lucy helped her with such projects and that the spirit was always in her room, watching over her.

Lucy may have been watching over Margaret, but she still loved to play pranks on the adults.

"She would move objects from one room to another," Sandra recalled. "She seemed to enjoy turning the electric lights on and off in empty rooms—and she loved to play the radio, however late at night."

They Learn How Lucy Fritch Passed to the Other Side

After several days, the lady at the local museum called and told Sandra that she and her staff had uncovered information about Lucy Fritch.

"In her physical life, Lucy had actually lived in the house next door," Sandra said. "At that time, about 1870 to 1875, our house had been owned by a physician, and Lucy, in her early twenties, had served as governess to his two children. She had fallen to her death from one of the floor-to-ceiling windows on the second floor to the ground below, about a forty-foot drop.

"The room from which Lucy had fallen was now our bedroom, the room where she had appeared to me," Sandra continued. "She had died from the accident about ninety-five years earlier."

Lucy Becomes a Cherished Companion for a Single, Pregnant Woman

Shortly after they had learned the earthlife identity of their spirit, Sandra hired Danielle, the daughter of their plant manager in New Orleans, to be her personal secretary.

"Danielle was single and pregnant," Sandra said. "I moved her into a private room in our haunted mansion. Well, sir, it didn't take long before Lucy moved in with her.

"Danielle didn't mind the company at all. In fact, she said it helped to have Lucy around to talk with and to be there so she had someone to whom she could cry out her troubles. Although Danielle was Cajun and had loved that backcountry music, Lucy even taught her to appreciate the classics."

In 1968, Danielle gave birth to a daughter, and when the baby was six weeks old, she moved back to New Orleans.

"Incredibly, after Danielle's baby was born, we never heard Lucy in the old house ever again," Sandra said.

Was Lucy Reborn to Live Again?

About a year and a half later, the Moores moved to Jackson, Mississippi. One evening they were having dinner at poolside when Danielle and her baby daughter surprised them by stopping in unannounced.

"I had not seen Danielle's baby since it was six weeks old," Sandra said. "Yet when they approached us on the patio, that child actually leaped out of Danielle's arms into mine. She started laughing, hugging, and kissing me all over my face. She clutched me tightly and kept looking into my face and kissing me.

"And then I realized *this was my Lucy!*" Sandra exclaimed, tears welling in her eyes. "The baby had light brown hair and blue eyes, as had Lucy.

"Lucy the friendly spirit had reincarnated as Danielle's child—and now she was so happy. And I had never been happier to see anyone. What a glorious reunion!"

The woman to whom we have given the name of Sandra Moore concludes her account by swearing that this is a true story. Lucy Fritch is the actual name of the friendly spirit who inhabited the Vicksburg mansion, but "Sandra" has asked that all other names of family and company personnel in the detailed report that she provided be changed. "Sandra" is now in her mid seventies and no longer resides in Mississippi.

"Prior to meeting Lucy, I would have been skeptical of anyone who told such a story as this or of anyone who claimed to believe in spirits," she concluded her account. "But I am so happy to learn that you have had such encounters, and it is your willingness to share them with others that prompted me to tell you this story."

4

BRINGING PEACE TO A HOUSE OF VIOLENT DEATH

I am frequently asked if I have ever been frightened during my paranormal investigations. Since I am not the hero of popular fiction but a real-life psychical researcher, I am certain that if I had been alone when I confronted some of the eerie manifestations that I have witnessed, I most surely would have been frightened. But nearly all of my investigations have been in the company of levelheaded police officers, journalists, and fellow psychical researchers. As I have stressed often, one should always be as well prepared as possible before setting out on any psychic safari into the unknown.

All that being said, certain of my journeys into the realm of the supernatural have haunted me in the sense that they seem to have touched me with a psychic residue that will occasionally surface in strange and unsettling dreams. In some instances, there seems almost to be a force that is calling me back to revisit the scene of some particularly baffling and eerie hauntings. It is as if I will be granted additional revelations if I return and allow the energy within these houses and places to permeate deeper levels of my psyche. Such a place would be the sprawling mansion in northern Minnesota that hovers just above the rocky shore of Lake Superior.

When I first received a call from the family currently residing in the home, it was readily apparent that the maelstrom of haunting activity in which they found themselves had driven them to the point of nervous exhaustion. At first the Rugland family could hardly believe their good fortune in acquiring the large house and estate at a ridiculously low price. But none of the real estate agents had bothered to tell them the place had been the scene of terrible murders and that it had been haunted for years.

"We moved here from Duluth," Lynne Rugland told me. "We had vacationed in a resort near here for years, and we just loved the heavy forested area and the access to the lake provided by the estate. It wasn't until we had moved in and the disturbances began that we began to ask some of the local inhabitants about the history of the place. Even then, only a few were willing to give us many details."

If Wayne Rugland had not become a successful architect who could afford to work out of his home and go into the office only once or twice a week, they would not have been able to realize their dream of living in the lovely forested area near Lake Superior some distance away from his firm in Duluth. "If only we had had some warning that our dream house would soon turn into a living nightmare," he said with an air of exasperation.

From what the Ruglands had been able to piece

together from local rumors and legends and the few residents who were willing to discuss the matter, the lumber and iron ore baron [we'll call him Karl Holtz] who had built the mansion in the 1890s had not married until he was well into his fifties. He had been far too busy accumulating an empire to take a bride and establish a family. And then, finally, after a brief courtship, he married a young woman barely in her twenties [Rebecca], summarily sired a son and heir [Milo], and continued his routine of leaving home on extended business trips.

Although Holtz doted on the boy whenever he was home, his young wife's lack of interest in high finance created an ever-widening breach between them—and her passion for painting and literature seemed silly and trivial to him. Even worse, Holtz was away from home far too long and too often to take notice of the growing affection between his bride and the young man from the village [Harold] whom he had hired to look after the estate in his absence.

As the Ruglands understood the history of the mansion, the emotional ingredients of a lonely, frustrated, neglected young wife who took a handsome groundskeeper as a lover combined to form the elements of classic melodrama—and murder. After many years of conducting a clandestine relationship, the two lovers plotted to bludgeon her husband while he slept, then toss his body to the rocks below the mansion and claim that he had accidentally fallen to his death.

On the night of a violent thunderstorm, Rebecca and Harold decided to put their plot into motion. They could testify that her husband, who was well known as one who loved watching the waves crash against the shore during storms, had slipped on the wet stone pathway to the lake and crushed his skull on the large, jagged boulders that lined the beach.

Shortly after midnight, the first step of the terrible plan had been achieved. Karl Holtz lay battered and bloody on his bed.

But then the couple's six-year-old son, awakened by the ghastly sounds of murder most foul, walked bleary-eyed into the awful scene and began to cry out in horror at the sight of his bleeding father lying sprawled amid the bedclothes.

As the story goes, Harold demanded that the young mother kill her son to shut him up. They couldn't leave any witnesses, he argued, and besides, he didn't want to bring up another man's child. They would have their own children once they were wed.

When Rebecca hesitated, her lover reminded her of their fears that Holtz had left all of his wealth and estate to his son in his will. Milo would have everything—and even if she could somehow convince the boy not to name them as his father's murderers, he would always be able to hold such a disclosure over their heads. They could be certain that, as he grew older, he would continue to keep them under his thumb, and they would become little more than his lackeys.

Her lover's argument convinced her to do the deed. Without another word of dissent, she dashed out the boy's brains with the same hammer that she had used to murder her husband. It would make their account of her husband's demise on the rocks all the more believable if his beloved son had been walking with him on the stone path to watch the crashing waves being churned up by the strong winds.

And now the tale takes an ironic twist. As the lovers were in the process of lifting the body of her husband to drop to the rocks below, Rebecca lost her footing and fell along with his corpse. She screamed out in pain and terror, her back quite likely broken, but before Harold could reach her, a series of waves pummeled the shore and pulled her out to drown in the depths of Lake Superior.

Confused and frightened, the groundskeeper fled the scene. He was apprehended three days later, not far from the Canadian border. Since he had no reasonable account of exactly how it was that his employer was found on the rocks near his home with his skull battered in and that his employer's son was found on the stone path above the beach with his own head crushed and that his employer's wife had completely vanished, it was not many months before the young man was found guilty of three murders and hanged by his neck until dead. Few people believed that the virtuous Rebecca had been involved with a common groundskeeper, and judge and jury discounted any of Harold's protestations that he had not killed anyone, that he had merely been a witness to his lover's crimes, and that Rebecca's own death had been accidental. His attorney attempted to get a lesser sentence out of the judge, such as conspiracy to commit murder or accessory to murder, but his halfhearted orations on his client's behalf indicated that he didn't really believe him.

Since that terrible and bloody night, the Ruglands learned, local residents had frequently sighted the ghostly form of a woman walking close to the large beach rocks near the mansion. Many witnesses stated that they could hear the spirit weeping and begging forgiveness for her sins. Harold's friends and relatives, several of whom were well aware of the young man's adulterous relationship with his employer's wife, swore that the spirit of Rebecca had been condemned to walk the rock-strewn beaches of Lake Superior because of her earthly misdeeds.

A few weeks after the murders, a man and his family, who had been hired by the millionaire's younger brother to look after the mansion until the estate could be settled, moved out, complaining of eerie and frightening occurrences. The man and his wife were the first to claim that they witnessed a spectral reenactment of the terrible murders and that they watched in horror as Rebecca raised her bloody hammer again and again to smash out the life of her husband and her son.

Over the years, the large, picturesque mansion had sat empty for long periods of time, but three families had tried to live there. One family lasted a year because they avoided entering the master bedroom. The others moved out in a matter of weeks or months— all claiming to have witnessed the grim, ghostly pageant play whenever there was a particularly violent thunderstorm. The house had been unoccupied for nearly nine years before the Ruglands bought the place from the original owner's great-nephew.

"We don't want to move out of the mansion," the Ruglands told me. "If it weren't for the ghosts, we love the place."

But they and their two sons, eleven-year-old Dean and seven-year-old Danny, didn't know how much longer they could tolerate the haunting phenomena that had begun to dominate their very existence.

The home seemed plagued by poltergeistic phenomena—objects being tossed about, furniture moving from its assigned positions, and so forth. The most frightening manifestation was that of a ghostly reenactment of the murders, which occurred in the master bedroom.

"Both times we witnessed the scene during a thunderstorm," Wayne said. "There are a lot of thunderstorms up here, and we don't care to see it ever again. We have now moved our bedroom downstairs."

I told the Ruglands that I would come to investigate the haunting with a team of researchers as quickly as possible. We agreed upon a date for our visit, and I instructed them to be certain that their young sons were not present during our examination of their home. Although I didn't explain to the Ruglands at the time, we had learned through past experiences that if we should decide to conduct an exorcism of sorts upon the home, it was best not to have impressionable children present.

Facing the Restless Spirits of the Holtz Mansion

On a sunny autumn day with just a touch of early October frost, I arrived at the mansion with my select team of investigators.

Audrey Gabrielson was a gifted psychic-sensitive, who, while not a "professional spirit medium," was an excellent channel for restless, earthbound entities. In addition, she was the mother of two sons and a daughter and was a well-balanced lady who had never given up her day job as an accountant.

My friend Mike Harris was a tough cop with a passion for metaphysics who, on his days off from the police department, loved to accompany me to detect suspects from the unseen world.

Janet Knutson, a local journalist who had herself investigated a number of hauntings on her own, had been the contact person who had given the Ruglands my unlisted telephone number. She was a tall woman with a warm and outgoing personality, an expert at setting nervous folks at ease.

When we arrived at the stately mansion nestled among birch and pine trees and standing like a sentinel atop the shoreline of Lake Superior, we found Lynne and Wayne Rugland waiting for us on the front porch. They wore ski jackets and sipped hot coffee to ward off the October chill.

"The manifestations have been especially bad today," Lynne told us by way of explanation for their meeting us outside the house. An attractive woman in her late thirties with strawberry-blond hair, she was dressed casually in jeans and a sweatshirt.

Wayne was obviously fighting anxiety over the circumstances in which his family found themselves. He was a tall, athletic man who probably always tried to project an image of being in control of the situation. It was immediately apparent that he was very uncomfortable with this new feeling of utter helplessness. His welcome smile was fleeting, a quick stretching of his lips.

"Maybe . . . they . . . the ghosts, that is . . . sensed that you were coming," he said, his laughter a nervous kind of coughing sound.

Janet laughed, lightly touching Wayne's sleeve. "Do you think the spooks have researcher radar?"

Audrey paused just before entering the mansion, her fingers brushing the ornate carvings on the doorway. "There are three spirits within," she said, as much to herself as to the rest of us. "Maybe more."

I was relieved that Audrey had dressed simply in a skirt and a sweater beneath her leather coat. She bore none of the stereotypical show business accoutrements of the spirit medium—no shawl, no voluminous skirt, no scarf or headband, no rows of multiple-colored beads, medallions, and charms— and there were just enough streaks of gray in her sensible brunette hairstyle to grant her an aura of mature wisdom. If Audrey had looked the least bit like Madame Maria Ouspenskaya portraying a gypsy seeress in an old Universal horror film, I am certain that the Ruglands would have freaked out.

We were astonished when we entered the spacious living room to observe that a number of the large couches bore blankets and pillows.

Noticing our puzzled expressions, Lynne explained that the family now slept downstairs. "We feel safer . . . more comfortable down here. The ghosts don't come down here quite as often."

As if to contradict her, a book launched itself from one of the shelves and struck her on her right thigh.

Wayne rushed to his wife's side, putting a protective arm around her shoulder.

Janet stepped forward to offer her concern, but I could tell by the way that the reporter bit her lower lip that she was silently cursing the fact that she hadn't managed to get a picture of the airborne object with her camera.

Lynne dismissed both her husband's solicitude and ours with a wave of her hand. "It didn't hurt," she smiled wanly. "Besides, I'm getting used to it."

Wayne told us that Lynne seemed to receive the brunt of such physical manifestations. She would be pelted with objects several times a day.

"I've never been injured, though," she emphasized. "But I was really frightened once when a steak knife stuck in the wall about six inches from my head."

I could see Audrey listening attentively to what was being said by the Ruglands—and I could also perceive her tuning into other voices that the rest of us did not hear. I waited for her to speak, but she chose to remain silent for the present.

Mike was checking the room out in his quiet, unobtrusive, experienced police officer's manner. From time to time, he would look up when someone spoke; then he would smile, nod his head, and return to "casing" the joint out.

Janet obtained permission to take some photographs of the room, and I decided to slip quietly upstairs to see if I could determine the house's "cold spot," a small area in a room or corridor that might be several degrees cooler than the rest of the place. Such areas were often indicators of precisely where the center of the haunting might be located.

A Most Unusual Little Boy

I was just starting to walk down the corridor at the top of the stairs when I saw a small boy, about six or seven, dart out of a room and run around the corner at the end of the hallway.

I became quite upset, because I had made it very clear to the Ruglands that their children must not be present when we came for our investigation of the house. The scampering child made it very obvious to me that either they had ignored one of the most important of my stipulations or the little rascal had crept back into the house of his own accord.

"I saw you, little man," I said. "You must go downstairs right away and leave the house."

The boy's head peeped back around the corner. He was very dark-complected with large brown eyes, eyes that looked at me sternly beneath furrowed brow. "This is my house," he said. "*You* leave!"

"Yes, yes," I answered impatiently. "But your mom and dad asked us here on business. Come with me downstairs right now."

The little head disappeared around the corner again, and I walked quickly down the corridor to apprehend the tiny interloper. I intended to take him by the hand and walk him downstairs to confront his parents.

But when I turned the corner, he was nowhere in sight. I decided that he had already beat it down a back stairway, so I went back downstairs to settle the matter with Lynne and Wayne.

"Where did you disappear to, Brad?" Janet, ever the inquisitive reporter, asked.

"I was just checking around upstairs," I asked, noticing the shocked expressions of the Ruglands.

"You went up alone?" Lynne wondered.

"Oh, I wasn't completely alone," I answered. Then, getting right to the point: "Lynne, Wayne, didn't I ask that neither of your sons be in the house when we came to investigate?"

Puzzled by my question, Wayne replied that both boys were with friends in the village.

"Well, then, I guess the younger guy, Danny, decided to come back home and check out what we were doing," I said. "I saw him upstairs, and I would greatly appreciate it if you would take him back to his friend's house."

Mike spoke up, echoing my edict. "We really don't want any kids around when we investigate a haunting."

Wayne turned very pale. "Danny's friend lives a good six, seven miles from here. There's no way he would walk back."

Lynne shook her head and her lower lip quivered when she told us: "Brad, you saw one of the ghosts. The little boy. Before we moved our sleeping quarters down here to the living room, he would often stand beside our bed at night and tell us that we were in his house, that we should leave."

I could not suppress the shiver that ran up my spine, but I wasn't convinced. I was certain that I had encountered a very real, very solid little boy upstairs.

And then Lynne was thrusting a framed photograph into my hands. "Look, here are Dean and Danny. Does either of them look like the little boy you saw upstairs?"

I was looking at two attractive boys. The older one, Dean, blond, blue-eyed; the younger, Danny, reddish-blond hair, with blue eyes smiling out of a freckled face.

"As you can see," Lynne continued, "our sons are light-haired and light-complected with blue eyes. The old stories have it that Rebecca, the woman who killed her son in this house, was of Chippewa-French background. The little boy ghost that we have seen is very dark. What about the little boy that you saw running down the upstairs hallway? Still think that he was Danny?"

"All right," I conceded. "I met your little ghost boy. And I'm tempted to say, 'In the flesh,' because he seemed that real."

Audrey laughed at my revelation that spirit entities can assume such natural and solid forms. "I think now we should all go upstairs," she said. "Brad can introduce us to his new little friend."

Wayne chuckled nervously. "If you folks lead the way, we'll follow."

Lynne held back, but Janet took one of her hands and squeezed it reassuringly. "C'mon," Janet whispered cheerily. "There's strength in numbers."

"Easy for you to say," Lynne said, managing a feeble smile. "I think the spooks really have it in for me."

The Little Ghost Boy Was Wary of the New Mother in the House

It appeared that Lynne was correct. When we entered the bedroom in which Dean and Danny had been sleeping, two plastic alphabet blocks and a small toy car seemed to catapult themselves at her.

Although she was struck once in the face and twice in her upper body, she again assured us that she was not injured. "They never hurt me. It just bothers me that I seem always to be their favorite target."

Audrey nodded. "The little boy . . ." She paused as if trying to select the most appropriate words to finish her sentence.

"I know," Lynne said, supplying her own interpretation of the medium's thoughts. "He doesn't like me."

Audrey shook her head. "It's not so much dislike as it is that he knows that you are the mother of this family. His mother betrayed him in the most horrible way that any mother could. He just plain distrusts mothers."

Wayne shook his head and tried to suppress an involuntary shudder. "The spirit of the boy was making contact with Danny," he said. "We knew it was happening. Dean saw the ghost in the room talking to Danny on several occasions."

"And that's when Danny started becoming rebellious, talking back to me, defying me," Lynne said.

"That's another reason we moved downstairs," Wayne said. "The boys never saw the horrible re-creation of the murders that we witnessed in the master bedroom during a couple of thunderstorms. They only knew that books, glasses, and other objects occasionally flew around the rooms and that a little spook sometimes came to visit them. To be honest, I think sometimes they actually thought it was kind of neat to have ghosts in the house."

It was Audrey's turn to shiver and express her concern. "That's not good. You don't want your kids getting scared out of their minds by spirits, but neither do you want them to be seduced. There is always a potential there for possession."

"Oh, God," Lynne gasped. "Possession!"

"Audrey doesn't mean the twisting neck and vomiting pea soup kind of possession," Mike was quick to explain. "She's talking about a more subtle kind of psychic union between the child and the spirit. Which can, of course, become hazardous to the child's mental health."

Mike's attempt at a more cautious interpretation of the relationship between a child and an earthbound spirit had no effect on Lynne. She had heard enough. "Wayne, we've got to get out of this house! Now!"

"Hold on, Lynne," Janet advised her. "You told me how much you loved this big, old place. You told me you didn't want to have the spooks drive you away. Remember, that's why I gave you Brad's telephone number."

Audrey reached out and took Lynne's hand. "Give us a chance to help the restless spirits find peace and their way into the Light."

Things That Go Bump in the Night

At that very moment, we were all startled by loud thumping noises overhead.

"The attic," Wayne said, glancing upward. "We often hear loud thumps and bumps coming from up there, especially after around ten or eleven at night."

Since it was a large walk-up attic, easily entered by a comfortable set of stairs, Mike bounded up the steps in an effort to catch the noisy ghosts in the act of disturbing the peace. "Nothing here," he called down after a few moments of seeking a source—ghostly or otherwise—for the thumping sounds.

"We've never seen anything, either," Wayne said. "I've checked for rats or squirrels, as well as ghosts. Even left some poison in the four corners of the attic, just in case I missed any critters trying to homestead up there."

Audrey wished to walk alone from room to room, permitting her psyche to pick up spirit vibrations without any distractions from the Ruglands or us.

"Do you think she'll conduct a spirit circle?" Janet asked me.

I answered that I thought it quite likely that she would.

"You mean a séance?" Wayne asked in a strained tone. "I read where séances can bring in evil spirits. We've got enough problems the way it is."

"There is no question that conducting séances is not for amateurs," Mike agreed with Wayne's concern. "There are disruptive spirits out there on the astral planes who could easily trick some would-be mediums, but Audrey is one of the very best. She won't allow any negative entities to come creeping in."

Lynne apologized for neglecting the laws of hospitality. "Can I offer anyone some coffee? And I made cinnamon rolls last night."

I accepted on behalf of our group. I felt allowing Lynne and Wayne to assume the traditional roles of hosts would help them to relax and to feel a bit more in control of their home environment.

After a brief coffee break spent in anxious bursts of small talk about any subject other than the haunting phenomena in their home and the approaching spirit circle to be conducted by Audrey, we adjourned to the upstairs master bedroom.

Conducting a Séance at the Scene of the Murders

"Understandably, the greatest concentration of spirit energy is in this room," Audrey explained. "The psychic atmosphere in here is exceedingly heavy and close—and dark. On the spirit level, the place reeks of violence, guilt, and betrayal. Terrible acts of greed, lust, and murder were committed here."

"Do we need to sit in a circle around a table?" Lynne wondered.

"That's not necessary," Audrey said. "I will lie down on that couch over there, and the rest of you bring chairs close to me so I may draw upon your energies."

Audrey lay down on the couch with her arms at her side as the five of us brought our chairs nearer. "From now on," she instructed us, "you don't call me Audrey. Throughout the séance, you call me 'the medium.' My chest is starting to get very heavy, and I can feel a powerful vibration in my hands and my body."

Audrey's voice suddenly became very hoarse, and she cleared her throat. "You can hear that my spirit guide, Dr. Matthews, is already starting to take control of my voice—and I'm not even in full trance yet. When Dr. Matthews arrives, speak only to him. If you see something happening or feel something happening in the room, please talk about it. Don't sit in silence. All right. I'm beginning to enter the trance state. I can feel my body becoming heavier and heavier . . ."

After a few moments of silence as the medium

went deeper into a trance state, the familiar soft, spectral voice of Dr. Benjamin Matthews, Audrey's principal spirit guide, addressed us: "Good evening, friends."

"Good evening, Dr. Matthews," our group of researchers greeted the spirit guide in unison. Wayne and Lynne followed our lead and softly whispered their own welcome. According to Audrey, Dr. Benjamin Matthews had been a wise, kind country doctor from Vermont until he was killed in 1863 while serving in the medical corps during the Civil War.

"I am very happy to be here this evening and to work with you in this manner," the spirit guide said. "Brad, I know that we have quite an agenda before us."

I acknowledged Dr. Matthews's appraisal of the situation, and I summarized the plight of the earthbound spirits in the Holtz mansion, who, for one reason or another, had not been able to find their way home into the Light.

"Ah, yes, the poor tormented spirits," Dr. Matthews said. "I see them clearly. I feel their anguish so strongly. I will not have to draw them out, for even now they crowd around us."

Lynne and Wayne glanced nervously over their shoulders.

"Yes, there are four such wretched spirits whom we must help go into the Light," Dr. Matthews declared.

I saw Janet frown and lift her fingers unconsciously as she mentally counted the spirits.

"Yes, Janet," Dr. Matthews told her. "Four. The spirit of one who was known on Earth as Karl Holtz is here, angry because he was taken suddenly from his material treasures and his great joy of accumulating even more wealth. The spirit of one named Rebecca is here, consumed with guilt for her terrible crimes. The spirit essence of little Milo is here, confused, not fully understanding that his spirit essence no longer occupies a physical body. He grieves because his mother deserted him. He has no memory of Rebecca's awful sacrifice of his life for her lover. Milo attempts to gain a surrogate mother whenever another woman moves into the mansion, and he becomes angry when they seem to ignore him."

"And the fourth?" Janet prompted when the spirit guide lapsed into a few moments of silence.

"Yes, the fourth spirit," Dr. Matthews sighed. "A most unfortunate and troubled entity named Harold. He has learned much on the Other Side, but he is still very disturbed and very earthbound."

Wayne was puzzled. "According to the accounts, Harold the groundskeeper was hanged about a hundred miles from here."

"There are no boundaries of time and space on this side," Dr. Matthews replied. "Harold's spirit has returned to this place because it was here that he sinned against his employer by engaging in an adulterous relationship with Rebecca, Karl's wife. It was here that he stood by and allowed Rebecca to murder both her husband and her beloved son. Although in life he attempted to argue his innocence before the laws of man, here he has learned that the acts of omission are as soul-damaging as the acts of commission."

We were all startled when Dr. Matthews's gentle description of the spirit world was suddenly replaced by a harsh, demanding, and much deeper voice:

"Who are you people? What are you doing in my house? Out, I say! Out at once!"

"Karl, please." Dr. Matthews once again assumed control over the medium's voice box. "This is no longer your home. You must now move on to your true home in the Light."

We could hear Karl Holtz's confused and angry muttering as he moved once again into the background.

"I will now pray for these poor, disturbed beings," Dr. Matthews said. "Please repeat aloud each sentence after I utter it:

O wondrous Beings of Light and Love, we call upon you to establish your protective energies around these four troubled earthbound spirits. O powerful Beings of Light and Love, erect a shield of holy energy around these earthbound spirits that is invincible and impenetrable. Surround them with a shield of holy energy that will erase all earthly concerns, all earthly desires, all earthly worries, all earthly emotions of anger, hate, and fear. O mighty Beings of Light and Love, accompany these earthbound spirits into the everlasting Light of All That Is. Grant them serenity in the kingdom of eternal harmony. Allow them to grow in wisdom and in grace and permit their eternal spirits to replace earthly memories of guilt, greed, and lust with heavenly thoughts of peace, love, and light. And now, O Beings of Light and Love, take these four unhappy earthbound spirits to their eternal home in the heavenly kingdom. *Take them now!*

There came soft sounds of sighs and moans from every corner of the master bedroom. Later, we all testified that we felt a rush of cold air as the four tormented spirits were taken to the Light by heavenly beings.

"I can feel it," Lynne said, tears moving freely down her cheeks. "I can feel a peace in the room."

Wayne agreed. "It's like the room . . . the entire house has a cleaner, purer, lighter atmosphere. Dear God, there's a new energy here!"

Before the spirit guide left us, he gave the Ruglands a special supplication to pray if they should ever again sense negative spirit energy in their home or anywhere around them:

Beloved Light Beings, place your protective energies around me at once. Place a shield of protection around me that is all-powerful, invincible, impenetrable. Keep me completely protected from all things that are not of the Light. Keep me safe from all negative vibrations. Surround me with the perfect love and eternal light of the Father-Mother-Creator Spirit.

We declined the Ruglands' generous offer to treat us to a special dinner at a very fine local restaurant. The hour was growing late, and we had more than a three-hour drive back to our homes. Although we were physically drained from the session, the knowledge that four tormented spirits had been led into the Light so lifted our hearts with joy that we probably had the energy to drive for twenty-four hours straight.

In follow-up telephone calls with the Ruglands, it

seemed as though Audrey's spirit guide had accomplished a most effective low-key exorcism of the Holtz mansion. Lynne and Wayne reported no additional negative manifestations in the magnificent old house. On occasion, they had glimpsed the image of Milo and once or twice the shimmering form of Rebecca, but the apparitions seemed more like photographs somehow projected against a wall. And there was absolutely no feeling of negativity or menace associated with the ethereal imagery. Once the nightmare elements of the haunting had been removed, the place truly had become their dream home.

So why is it that from time to time my own dreams take me back to the darkened corridors of the Holtz mansion?

In a night vision often repeated, Wayne, Lynne, and Audrey are standing beside me as I hold a small, ornate chest in my hands. I want to open the treasure chest, but I hear a warning voice from Spirit advising me to keep it closed. I think I understand the dream's symbolic meaning.

I so often recall the image of the little ghost boy that I encountered in the Holtz mansion. When I assumed that he was a child of flesh, he responded to my demand that he leave the house by saying that *I* should be the one to go. I am tormented by the fact that I blew my chance to have an actual dialogue with a spirit. If I had realized that the little boy was a ghost, I might have been able to open a veritable "treasure chest" of opportunity to ask all the great questions that have plagued humankind since our species first began to wonder about life after death.

With its remarkable variety of haunting phenomena, the Holtz mansion could have become a "treasure chest" of the paranormal. If we had not been so successful in sending its four restless spirits into the Light, we might have turned the place into a virtual living laboratory of the supernatural and discovered many gateways to the Other Side. On the other hand, we might have opened a Pandora's box by doing so. We might have become seduced by the dark side of the unknown and allowed the Ruglands' dream house to become an even more hellish nightmare than we found it.

Those pledged to spiritual work must always have as their principal goal the rendering of service to those who ask assistance in finding their way through the shadowy maze of the supernatural. My spirit teacher wouldn't want me to behave in any other way.

5

MEETING YOUR SPIRIT TEACHER

My first physical encounter with my spirit teacher ranks high among the life-altering events of my sojourn on planet Earth.

I was awakened one night in 1972 by an unusual kind of buzzing sound, and to my horror, I sat up to encounter a hooded figure at my bedside.

In the dim light issuing through the curtains from an outside streetlight, I could see that the unexpected bedroom intruder, who looked very much like a cowled monk, was waving his arms over me in a peculiar manner.

Interpreting his movements as threatening, I was instantly wide-awake. I rolled out of bed, stood up, and prepared to deliver as solid a punch as I could manage right into the face of the person who had invaded our home.

Whatever his intentions, we would sort them out right after I clobbered him. I was a man protecting my sleeping wife and four kids. And even if the intruder turned out to be a monk from some religious order, he should learn to knock—not break into someone's home and creep around in the dark.

Although I began my roundhouse punch, my blow never landed. I felt all the strength drain from my body and my arms dropped limply to my sides.

This was back in my iron-pumping, jogging days. I was doing bench presses and curls. I was strong.

But at that moment, I had never felt so weak, so helpless in my life.

I collapsed in a heap back on the bed. I remember that I actually began to weep in fear and confusion. I was completely at the mercy of whoever or whatever had come into our bedroom.

It was then that the hooded being spoke. *"Don't be afraid,"* he said in a quiet whisper. *"We* [or he] *won't hurt you."*

And the next thing I knew the morning sunlight was making me squint into wakefulness.

There was no physical trace that a hooded entity or anyone else had been in our bedroom during the night, but strangely, within my mind there had been planted the seed of an idea for a book about the contemporary revelatory experience.

Had it all been a strange dream?

I had dreamed concepts for books before, but I had a peculiar kind of feeling that the visit of the cowled monk was not simply a character in a bizarre night-time vision meant to inspire me.

As I reflected on the incident throughout the day, I became more and more convinced that some kind of actual visitation had occurred and that some kind of actual physical entity had come to our bedroom in the wee hours before dawn.

The Hooded Entity Returns on the Following Night

The next evening, I was just falling asleep when I became aware of a peculiar buzzing that sounded for all the world like the noise a metallic bumblebee might make.

I realized at once that it was just such a sound that had awakened me the night before when the cowled being invaded our bedroom.

I was instantly wide-awake. Could it possibly be that the entity was returning for another visit?

When I focused my attention on the open door to the bedroom, I perceived a greenish-colored light emanating from somewhere in the stairway.

My pulse quickened as I saw a green globe of softly glowing light moving down the hallway toward our bedroom.

On one level of consciousness I knew that somehow the glowing orb was associated with the hooded entity. Somehow I knew that at any moment the greenish globe of light would transform itself into the cowled, monklike figure. The being was returning for some purpose I had not yet completely ascertained.

But I resolved that on this, his second visit, I would not under any circumstances allow him to "knock me out," the way he had done on the preceding visitation. I would stay alert and mentally analyze every moment of the experience.

And I would ask my uninvited visitor a host of questions concerning his identity, his place of origin, and the reason for these nocturnal encounters.

The greenish globe entered the bedroom, hovered near the bedside, and this time I heard a deep, but very pleasant, male voice command me: *"You will listen!"*

I perceived only a glimpse of the hooded figure as he somehow extricated himself from the glowing orb; then, at once, my physical self and my questioning brain were silenced.

Once again, my next conscious memory was that of the morning sunlight streaming through the bedroom windows.

But aha! What incredible thoughts had been fed directly into my unconscious mind! I now had bursting within the creative corridors of my psyche the passionate conviction that my next book was to be about the experiences of men and women who had entered into spiritual contact and communication with a Higher Intelligence. And I knew that I would entitle the book *Revelation: The Divine Fire.*

I also realized that my cowled after-midnight visitor had not come to frighten me, but to inspire me. Once he had silenced my nonstop questioning mind, he had placed me in a receptive kind of trance and provided me with the idea for an exciting new project.

In addition to the theme and general outline of the book, he had also placed within my psyche a number of relevant and useful names of men and women who would make excellent contributions to the power and worth of the text.

The mysterious entity who had materialized in my

bedroom was neither restless spirit nor alien intruder, but my very own spirit teacher.

Revelation: The Divine Fire was published in 1973 by Prentice-Hall, and it immediately became one of the most important and significant works that I have produced. Wherever I have lectured or presented seminars in the past twenty-eight years, there has been a number of individuals who will testify that that particular book was the one that turned their lives around or that gave them the spiritual tools that they required at that particular time to restructure their lives in a more positive direction.

I can only take credit for having been a competent stenographer for the book. *Revelation: The Divine Fire* was given to me by my spirit teacher as an important contribution to the accomplishment of my mission on Earth.

The Spirit Teacher Returns Eight Years Later and Reveals His Name

It was nearly eight years later before the hooded figure appeared to me again. This time I was permitted to remain conscious as my spirit teacher presented me with the exact information for which I had been seeking to complete a very important project. He also told me that his name was Elijah

About a year later, Elijah, my cowled spirit mentor, came to me when I was suffering with painful boils and skin eruptions that covered a good portion of my body. I was in a situation where I was unable to seek proper medical attention, and I lay naked and miserable on my bed, unable to bear even the touch of a sheet on my skin.

Taking pity on my woeful physical condition, Elijah gave me specific instructions to ingest a certain rather bizarre combination of ordinary foods and to do so immediately. My rational mind protested that the mixture might make me feel even worse, but I had faith in my ethereal guardian and teacher.

I staggered out of bed, ingested the prescribed mixture, and within two or three hours, all traces of the swellings had vanished from my body, never to return.

In 1987, a most important visitation from my spirit counselor occurred in my apartment in Scottsdale, Arizona, when Elijah confirmed that Sherry Hansen was the one with whom I was to walk together on a mutually rewarding spiritual and physical lifepath in order to carry out our respective assignments on Earth.

Such Spirit Teachers Are Sent, Not Summoned

At this point I must emphasize that I have no secret or magical method of commanding my spirit teacher to appear to me to help me out of some idiotic mess that I have created for myself through careless mistakes or woeful misjudgments. Nor would I ever pray to my spirit teacher to materialize and come to my assistance. I pray only to God, the Father-Mother-Creator Spirit, All That Is.

In truth, I have absolutely no way to determine

when my hooded teacher will appear physically before me. I am only grateful when he chooses to do so.

I very much agree with those spiritual counselors and teachers—my wife among them—who admonish us that spirit teachers and angelic messengers are *sent* to us, rather than *summoned* by us. I think that those who attempt to invoke the presence of such spirit beings are treading very close to Dark Side magic and that the entity who appears in answer to your invocations may most likely be an opportunistic creature from the Dark Side who will gleefully misguide you under the pretense of doing your bidding.

That being said, I *do* believe that we can employ certain meditations, prayers, and spiritual exercises that may encourage the proper *attitude* and *spiritual environment* to prompt visitations from our guides and teachers so that we may feel or sense their presence.

On numerous occasions, after prayer or meditation, I am very much aware of the presence of my spirit teacher near me. I have no need to see Elijah physically, for I feel a great sense of peace surround me that I know emanates from All That Is and is focused through his spiritual energy. Over the nearly thirty years since he first materialized before me, I have been content with knowing that Elijah's loving energy is pulsating interdimensionally and touching my being with a blessed harmony that will always connect our spirits.

So I do believe in utilizing those spiritual techniques that very often electrify the very atmosphere of the room with an almost palpable energy of unconditional love and heavenly tranquility. These exercises should, however, be practiced only with the goals of attaining spiritual guidance and awareness or peace and harmony, never with the desire of achieving anything of a material nature.

Utilizing the Mental Mechanism of a Spirit Teacher to Accelerate Spiritual Progress

In the period from 1974 to 1987, I worked extensively with a series of creative visualizations and relaxation techniques that I had specially designed to enable individuals to develop their awareness of higher states of consciousness. During these one-on-one sessions, I found that by permitting my subjects to envision their spirit teacher, I had created an extremely effective technique which would enable them to move farther and faster on the path of their spiritual progress. To accomplish this, I employed a creative visualization that *simulated* an encounter with one's spirit teacher, who then led the subject on an inner voyage of discovery.

Admittedly, most men and women who came to me for metaphysical counseling already believed in the existence of benevolent multidimensional beings that would guide and protect them. But when a young woman arrived in my office who openly declared herself an atheist who had no time for thoughts of a Supreme Being, angels, or spooks, I soon discovered that whether or not the theory of spirit guides fits into one's prior cosmology was unimportant.

This particular client had been sent to me by a psychiatrist who had been unable to hypnotize her and had therefore been unable to begin an effective therapy. Although the psychiatrist practiced in New York and I lived in Phoenix at that time, he had heard of my relaxation techniques and felt that I might be able to assist his client to achieve a successful altered state of consciousness.

Indeed, when I explained to the somewhat hostile young woman that she could perceive her spirit guide as a trustworthy friend with special abilities and unique insights, or as an evolutionary archetype within her own higher consciousness—an older, wiser aspect of herself—she accepted the concept on an intellectual level. Once she had come to terms with her spirit guide as an older, wiser aspect of her own psyche, I was successful in placing her into a very deep altered state of consciousness within a very short time.

What I learned from this experience was that even when employed solely as a mental mechanism, the concept that one has a special spirit teacher—or spiritual companion of some kind—is extremely effective in enabling one to gain the kind of confidence and self-assurance that is especially valuable in achieving contact with a source of inspiration outside—or inside—oneself.

While I firmly believe that wonderful experiences and encounters with a spirit teacher are available for every sincere seeker, I stress that even if your personal beliefs permit you to consider such entities only as creations of your own psyche, the mechanism itself will work for you in achieving valuable insights into your strengths and weaknesses.

Preparing to Undergo
a Relaxation Technique

I am now going to present a relaxation technique that I have employed with great success in working with hundreds of individual clients and, on occasions at special seminars, with audiences of over a thousand men and women.

If you allow yourself to follow the technique, it will place you in a receptive state of consciousness that will enable you to establish a spiritual linkup with your spirit teacher, or a more aware aspect of your psyche.

It is possible for you to read this relaxation technique, pausing occasionally to permit its effectiveness to permeate your spiritual essence. You may stop every now and then to contemplate the significance of your inner journey and to receive an elevation to a higher state of consciousness.

It may be even more helpful to have another serious-minded person slowly read the technique to you, following the instructions carefully.

Others have found it extremely effective to read this technique into a cassette recorder and to play the tape back, allowing their own voice to guide them through the exercise.

Any of these methods can be effective. Your success will depend upon your willingness to permit such an experience to manifest in your conscious mind.

It is important that before you begin this exercise you have isolated at least fifty minutes in your schedule when you know that you will not be interrupted.

You may sit up or lie down during the process, whichever position you find the most comfortable.

Many who have successfully used this technique have played soft music in the background to intensify the effect. Be certain, however, that whatever music you might choose contains absolutely no lyrics. Any lyrics, regardless of how inspirational, will be certain to distract you from the desired goal of the exercise.

Some of my students who have utilized this relaxation technique and achieved marvelous results have preferred to play a recording of ocean waves in the background.

The Relaxation Technique

Now, sit or lie down. Take three comfortably deep breaths . . . and begin:

See yourself lying on a blanket on a beautiful stretch of beach. You are lying in the sun or in the shade, whichever you prefer.

You are listening to the sounds of Mother Ocean. You are listening to the rhythmic sound of the waves as they gently lap against the shore. You are listening to that same restful lullaby that Mother Ocean has been singing to men and to women for thousands and thousands of years.

As you relax, you know that nothing will disturb you, nothing will distress you, nothing will molest or bother you in any way.

Even now you are becoming aware of a golden light of love, wisdom, and knowledge that is moving over you, protecting you. You know that you have nothing to fear. Nothing can harm you. This is the light of God's love moving over you.

As you listen to the soft, soothing lullaby of the ocean waves, you feel all tension leaving your body.

The sound of the waves helps you to become more and more relaxed. With every breath you take, you find yourself becoming more and more relaxed.

You are now feeling a beautiful energy of tranquility, peace, and love entering your feet . . . and you feel every muscle in your feet relaxing . . . relaxing.

And the beautiful energy of tranquility, peace, and love moves up your legs, into your ankles, your calves, your knees, your thighs . . . and you feel every muscle in your ankles, your calves, your knees, your thighs relaxing, relaxing, relaxing.

If you should hear any sound at all other than the ocean waves and the voice that is now speaking to you, you will not be disturbed.

If you should hear any other sound at all—a slamming door, a honking horn, a shouting voice—that sound will not disturb you. That sound will actually help you to relax even more.

And now that beautiful energy of tranquility, peace, and love is moving up to your hips, your stomach, your back . . . and you feel every muscle in your hips, your stomach, your back relaxing, relaxing, relaxing.

And with every breath you take, you find that your body is becoming more and more relaxed.

Now the beautiful energy of tranquility, peace, and love enters your chest, your shoulders, your arms, your fingers . . . and you feel every muscle in your chest, your shoulders, your arms, your fingers relaxing, relaxing, relaxing.

And with every breath you take, you find that you are becoming more and more relaxed. Every part of your body is becoming free of stress and tension.

Now that beautiful energy of tranquility, peace, and love moves into your neck, your face, the top of your head . . . and you feel every muscle in your neck, your face, and the top of your head relaxing, relaxing, relaxing.

Meeting Your Spirit Teacher: The Process

Your body is now relaxed, relaxed, relaxed. But your mind—your True Self—is aware. Your True Self has reached a very, very high level of consciousness.

And now you see a beautiful golden globe of light moving toward you. You are not afraid, for you understand, you *know*, that within the globe of light is your spirit teacher, the very being who has loved you since *before* you became you on an earthly mission.

Feel the love as this spiritual presence comes closer to you. Feel the vibrations of unconditional love moving over you—warm, peaceful, tranquil. You know that within this globe of light is a being who has always loved you just as you are and has always been present to assist you on your true mission to Earth.

On some level of consciousness, ever since you were a small child, you have always been aware of this loving, guiding presence in your life. You have always been aware that this intelligence has loved you just as you are . . . no facades, no masks, no pretenses.

Now you feel that heavenly, unconditional love moving all around you.

And look! Two eyes are beginning to form in the midst of the golden light. See the eyes of your spirit teacher. Feel the love flowing to you from this loving being.

Now a face is forming. See the beautiful smile on the lips of your spirit teacher.

Feel the love that flows from this wonderful being.

Now a body is forming. You may see your spirit teacher as male or female.

Behold the magnificence of form, structure, and stature of your spirit teacher. *Feel* the love that flows to you from the very presence of your spiritual instructor.

Your spirit teacher is now stretching forth a loving hand to you. Take that hand in yours. Accept your spirit teacher's hand in yours.

Feel the love flowing through you at the very touch of your spirit teacher's hand.

Feel the love as you and your spirit teacher blend and flow together as one.

You now know clearly that you have help always available to you whenever life on the earthplane becomes stressful and painful.

You know without question that you have a spirit teacher to work with you in achieving the goal for which you put on the fleshly clothes of a human being.

You know that you have always with you the power of the unseen presence of your spirit teacher.

And now your spirit teacher will speak to you and allow you to hear clearly its name. When your spirit teacher gives its name, you will hear it clearly.

Listen. Your spirit teacher is speaking to you now.

Hear the words your teacher speaks:

You will be always aware that I am with you, regardless of the storms and stresses which you must face on Earth. You may call upon my name for strength and comfort whenever you feel you need to feel my presence near you. Know and understand that I am always here to help you fulfill your mission on Earth.

My name is [*pause here for about fifteen seconds to allow the subject to hear clearly the name of his or her spirit teacher*].

You have now clearly heard the name of your spirit teacher. You know that you may call upon this name whenever you feel the need for positive reinforcement, for comfort, for courage.

You know you may feel the vibration of unconditional love whenever you feel the need for the support of a love that is eternal and everlasting.

You understand that you may call upon your spirit teacher whenever you need heavenly energy in fulfilling your assignment on planet Earth.

And now with all these glorious, heavenly images of your spirit teacher and the name of your teacher firmly in your mind, you feel yourself returning to full conscious awareness.

At the count of five, you will return to full consciousness feeling better than you have felt in months and months. You will return to full consciousness feeling more aware than you have ever felt in your life.

One . . . coming awake and feeling filled with unconditional, heavenly love and with greater awareness of your mission on Earth.

Two, coming more and more awake, clearly aware of your spirit teacher's name, face, and form.

Three, more awake, stretching your arms and legs, more clearly focused on the fulfillment of your earthly mission.

Four, more and more awake, filled with love, wisdom, and knowledge.

Five . . . wide-awake and feeling wonderful!

6

THE OTHER FACE IN THE MIRROR

Near-death and out-of-body experiences frequently open doorways to the supernatural realm; and all too often those who undergo such soul journeys and soar free of time and space on the Other Side are completely unprepared for where they may travel—and whom or *what* they may encounter. One thing we must never forget: the world of the supernatural is home to creatures of darkness as well as beings of light.

John W. White, one of the founders of the International Association for Near-Death Studies, calls the near-death experience a "crash course in spirituality and the human potential to expand consciousness." Reflecting upon his own near-death experience (NDE) at the age of fourteen for our *Children of the Light: The Startling and Inspiring Truth About Children's Near-Death Experiences*, White commented:

> [The near-death experience] introduced me to the power of consciousness and the hidden di-

mensions of human life. Since then I have experienced deeper, fuller spontaneous alterations of consciousness that have impelled me to practice more deliberate means for expanding awareness, realizing ultimate values, and maturing in character. But the seed energy of that NDE was planted and grew.

What White is saying is that while undergoing a near-death experience does not provide the earthly pilgrim with the ultimate burst of spiritual enlightenment, it nearly always serves as a profound revelation of the "hidden dimensions" that await more complete and deeper explorations.

I am certain that a good many readers will be familiar with the commonality of the kinds of experiences that a near-death survivor undergoes. Many researchers have established a kind of pattern profile of the NDE which includes the following:

At the moment of near-death, percipients generally report a life review and envision themselves floating out of their bodies and moving down a dark tunnel toward a brilliant light source. Very often they state that they encountered the spirits of deceased friends and relatives or were accompanied in their journey by a holy figure or a Light Being. When they are told they must return to their bodies, the survivors of NDEs are frequently disappointed and wish to remain on the Other Side.

Projecting the Spiritual Essence Out of the Body

Spontaneous out-of-body experiences (OBEs) are those instances in which the spirit, the mind, the very essence of a human being has been projected outside of the physical body to locations as near as the other side of a room or across the country or into another plane of existence and been able to return with conscious memories of the experience.

In such stress and pain situations as the moment of an accident, certain individuals have seemingly transcended the boundaries of time and space. Others, during acute illness and suffering, have testified to having traveled in other dimensions of reality. There exist the testimonies of thousands of men and women who have claimed to have seen the spiritlike image of a friend or a relative appear before them while the actual living, physical counterpart of the apparition was known to be thousands of miles away. Numerous individuals have undergone OBEs during sleep and have witnessed activities during their strange "dreams" that have been later verified. Some dream travelers state that they receive or convey messages of great personal importance during an out-of-body experience.

The experiences of those who have left the material body before death should only serve further to demonstrate that there is a nonphysical human capacity that cannot be made subject to the limitations which form a boundary around us when we exist as physical humans.

Psychical researcher Frederic W.H. Myers termed out-of-body experiences the most extraordinary achievement of the human will. "What can lie further outside any known capacity than the power to cause a semblance of oneself to appear at a distance?" Myers wondered. "What can be more a central action—more manifestly the outcome of whatsoever is deepest and most unitary in man's whole being? Of all vital phenomena, I say, this is the most significant; this self-projection is the one definite act which it seems as though a person might perform equally well before and after bodily death."

Dr. Hornel Hart's research led him to contend that the brain was but an instrument by which consciousness expresses itself, rather than a generator which produces consciousness. Dr. Hart felt that the evidence strongly supports the testimonies of those who feel that the "essential core" of personal consciousness might observe and act at long distances away from the brain.

Some researchers have estimated that 25 percent of the U.S. population have undergone some kind of out-of-body experience and at least 15 percent have returned to the physical body after a near-death experience. The statistics of our *Steiger Questionnaire of Paranormal, Mystical, and UFO Experiences*—which we began distributing to readers of our books and members of our lecture audiences in 1967, men and women interested in exploring the individual mystical experience—show that 76 percent claim OBEs and 57 percent NDEs.

In my opinion, spontaneous OBEs seem to fit into one of six general categories:

1. Projection while the subject sleeps.
2. Projection while the subject is anesthetized while

undergoing surgery, childbirth, tooth extraction, and so forth.

3. Projection at the time of an accident, during which the subject receives a terrible physical jolt and seems to have his or her spirit literally thrown from the material body.

4. Projection during intense physical pain.

5. Projection during severe illness.

6. Conscious out-of-body projection in which the subject deliberately seeks to catapult the spirit from the physical body.

The Hazards of Conscious Out-of-Body Projections

It is during attempts to practice Number 6, conscious OBEs, commonly referred to as "astral projections," that a lot of earnest, but inexperienced, metaphysical practitioners find themselves in trouble. In his classic work *Astral Projection: A Record of Out-of-Body Experiences*, Oliver Fox is explicit about the risks involved in conscious mind projections. He emphasizes that those with weak hearts and nervous conditions must never attempt deliberate OBE. In addition, Fox listed such dangers as temporary misalignment of the etheric body with the physical body, severance of the spirit mechanism that links the soul with the material body, and obsession.

After naming many other such dire possibilities as heart failure and insanity, Fox admits that it is his personal belief that experiments in conscious, deliberate mind travel are really no more dangerous than driving an automobile. He is also convinced that "unseen intelligences," that is, one's guardian and guides, stand ever ready to lead the neophyte experimenters back to their bodies.

"The great danger in an inexperienced individual attempting a conscious out-of-body projection lies in spirit possession," a medium once said to me as we discussed astral projection. "There are spirits who remain earthbound and who are still desirous of inhabiting a physical body. Some of these wretched souls feel that they have left too many tasks undone and they desire another fleshly body and another opportunity to complete their labors on the earthplane.

"And there are always evil entities which one must truly be on guard against during the projection experience," the medium continued. "These creatures of darkness are always seeking a passive, living body to invade and inhabit. That is why a medium, such as myself, always conducts a séance in an attitude of prayerfulness. Before I go into trance, I will ask God for protection and alert my spirit guide to guard me against these malignant influences."

A Conscious Projection Attracts a Spirit Parasite

Seventeen-year-old Jolene Kozisek, a passionate student of the paranormal and the occult, had the will and enthusiasm to experiment with conscious out-of-body projections, but unfortunately she had neglected to assume a prayerful attitude and to alert her spirit guide to guard her against malignant influences.

Her parents, Darwin and Aileen, called me to their home after a Friday night slumber party encounter with an Ouija board had left their daughters, Jolene and Joy, and three of their friends in hysterics.

According to Jolene, it had all begun three nights before on Tuesday evening after she had achieved a successful out-of-body projection. The teenager said that everything was going according to her usual procedure and she was in the process of returning to her physical body when she became aware of a dark presence following her.

"At first it seemed something like a dark cloud," she said. "Or maybe even some kind of dark cloth, like a billowing cloak of some kind."

Immediately after reentering her body, she fell into a deep sleep.

"But when I awakened sometime before morning, I had an awful feeling," she said. "It felt like something icky was in the room with me."

Jolene got up, turned on all the lights in her bedroom, and went to the bathroom. "The lights made things better," she recalled, "so I just left them on until it was time for me to get up and go to school."

Wicked Thoughts and Actions Not Her Own Beset Her

But even during the day at high school, she felt peculiar. "Really weird and nasty thoughts kept popping into my mind," she said. "Stupid thoughts, ugly thoughts—and especially sexual thoughts. I found myself fantasizing about guys—and girls. I saw myself in sexual situations with guys that I had never before even found the least bit attractive. And when I walked between classes with my boyfriend, Jake, I was literally trembling from the sexy feelings that I had for him."

At lunchtime in the cafeteria, Jolene's friends teased her for the gusto with which she consumed the same menu that was her usual butt of gross wisecracks. "They laughed at the way I was scarfing down the macaroni and cheese and lime Jell-O and finishing anything that was left on their plates," she said. "They joked that my parents must not be feeding me at home. I couldn't believe it myself. I usually made up gross and disgusting names for the stuff they fed us in the cafeteria. That day, it all tasted so good I couldn't seem to get enough."

She behaved in a similar manner with her mother's meatloaf and mashed potatoes that evening at home. Jolene remembers her parents reprimanding her for apparently having forgotten her table manners and for eating like a pig. Her twelve-year-old sister Joy giggled and asked her if she wanted a trough.

Later that night, as Jolene prepared for bed, she washed her face, applied some cold cream on her face, and was in the process of her evening "zit check" in front of her bathroom mirror when she found herself becoming completely fascinated with her features.

"It was as if I was seeing myself for the first time," she said. "Suddenly my nose, my cheekbones, my lips, my chin, my long dark hair—all of me seemed so totally wonderful. I was really beautiful. I wasn't just all right—I was terrific. And especially my eyes. I found myself just staring into the reflection of my eyes in the mirror."

Jolene has no idea how long she stood mesmerized by her own image in the mirror before she was aware of Joy standing beside her and squealing in disgust: "Eeeew! You really love yourself, don't you, Miss Movie Star? How creepy can you get? You were about to kiss yourself in the mirror!"

Jolene screamed at her sister, reminding Joy how many times she had forbidden her from entering "Her Majesty's" room without knocking first and gaining permission to do so.

"But the little Smurf was right," Jolene admitted. "It was creepy the way I was standing there just staring at myself."

Unusually Powerful ESP Abilities Manifest

It became even creepier and more disconcerting when Jolene was brushing her teeth on Wednesday morning and saw a few moments of a fleeting "motion picture" in the mirror.

"It was like the mirror became a kind of crystal ball," she said, "and I saw my boyfriend, Jake, and his buddy Chuck getting in a fender bender on the way to school that morning. When Jake wasn't in his homeroom, I knew that I had seen true. By third hour, everyone was talking about the accident. I had received an accurate prevision of an actual future event."

For the first time, Jolene decided to share her uncomfortable experience with the shadowy form that followed her back to her body during the OBE. Melanie, Heather, and Michaela were three close friends who were also fascinated by the supernatural. All four of them were fans of the various vampire slayers and witches on television, and each of them had built up a small library of books on magic, witchcraft, and the occult.

"Melanie hoped one day to become an initiated witch," Jolene said. "Heather experimented with a lot of different areas of the paranormal, and Michaela wanted to study to be a parapsychologist when she entered college."

Jolene told them that not only had she foreseen Jake and Chuck's accident that morning, but ever since that night she had been receiving other kinds of strange visions.

"I could tell they really got off when I told them about all the sexual fantasies that had come to me, but they were most impressed with my ability to pick up impressions from some of the jewelry and stuff they had. I told them where they had got certain items or who had given it to them. Things I swear I didn't know before."

Then Michaela, the budding parapsychologist, removed the deck of miniature Zener cards that she always carried in her purse. The deck consists of five each of five symbols—the square, the cross, the wavy lines, the circle, and the star—and is used to test ESP.

"The girls were totally amazed when I first got twenty out of twenty-five right, then twenty-two and twenty-three out of twenty-five," Jolene said. "Before when Michaela had tested me, I had never got too much above chance, five, six, or seven correct."

The consensus of Jolene's confidantes was that an entity from the Other Side had somehow managed to follow her home and was granting her increased psychic powers, such as an ability to receive glimpses of the future.

"I could tell that they were all kind of jealous of me, you know," Jolene said.

A Frightening Image Appears in Her Mirror

When Jolene looked into the mirror that night, she was startled to see a face behind her own, just to the left of her shoulder. "The image really frightened me," she said. "It looked a lot like me, but its eyes had dark rings around them. Its hair was stringy, and its complexion had a kind of greenish tint to it. And when it smiled at me, it seemed more like an evil leer."

Jolene dropped to her knees and began to utter a prayer for protection and a supplication that she be surrounded by a shield of Light. If only she had included such prayers in her regular out-of-body experiments, she quite likely would not have found herself in the company of an unbidden guest from the Other Side.

"After I had completed my prayers for protection and the banishment of evil, the mirror was once again clear," Jolene said. "I hoped that I had sent the thing back where it belonged and far away from me."

Things might have been resolved and the entity discouraged by Jolene's fervent prayers if the next day over lunch in the cafeteria Heather hadn't suggested that the four of them conduct a séance with the Ouija board to see if they could learn the identity of the entity who had followed her home.

"I tried to warn them that this thing looked really evil and that we should let it go back to the Other Side," Jolene said. "But Heather kept insisting what a great research project this could be, and she got Michaela all excited about a big experiment, and pretty soon Melanie had come on board.

"I really began to suspect that Heather's motives were not strictly academic, you know. I think if truth were told, she was jealous when the entity appeared to have granted me these big ESP powers, and she wondered if she might not be able to channel and control such energy if we worked some more with the being."

Against Jolene's objections, it was agreed that Friday night would be Ouija board night at her house. It was Jolene's turn to host a slumber party anyway, so her parents wouldn't suspect that anything unusual might be occurring under their roof.

The Koziseks had been given a clue, however.

A Strange Encounter with His Daughter's Double

Darwin told me that on Wednesday evening as he came up the stairs to go to bed, he thought he saw Jolene in the hallway outside her room.

"I called to her to ask her what she was doing up at that late hour on a school night, but she didn't answer me," he said. "As I approached her, she turned and entered her bedroom. When I opened the door to see if anything were troubling her, I was surprised to see her in bed, quite obviously fast asleep."

And then Darwin Kozisek received a couple of other surprises. "I thought I caught a glimpse of her standing in the doorway of her bathroom," he recalled. "How could this be? I wondered, because she is lying right there in her bed, right in front of me. And then I thought I saw the glowing outline of another person standing in the shadows off to the right of Jolene's bed. There was a soft, hissing sound from the direction of the bathroom, and where I thought I had seen Jolene, there was now only darkness."

Darwin left his older daughter's room convinced that his eyes had been deceived by patterns of light and shadow. He had been working too hard, staying up too late, and suffering from sleep deprivation— all of which had caused him to see things that weren't there.

The trouble was, the "things" really were there.

The Psychic Disaster of the Slumber Party Séance

The slumber party seance quickly became a psychic disaster. Twelve-year-old Joy begged to be included, and Michaela agreed, stating that a child's openness toward such matters could very likely provide the circle with greater energy.

At the stroke of midnight, they began their attempts to contact the entity that had attached itself to Jolene during her out-of-body projection. All the girls knew from watching various television programs and reading certain books on the occult that midnight was the "witching hour," the time when doorways to the unknown opened a bit wider.

At first the planchette under the girls' fingertips moved smoothly from letter to letter on the Ouija board, blithely spelling out a quaint tale of a young seamstress named Suzette who had been killed by runaway horses in the streets of their city in the 1880s. Her spirit had remained earthbound for many years, pining for her love, Raymond, who remained devoted to her memory.

Just as the five girls were growing teary-eyed over the sad tale of a young woman deprived of life and love by a cruel accident, the board suddenly began to spell out lewd descriptions of Suzette and Raymond's sexual techniques. At once repulsed and fascinated, the girls were soon learning how the spirit of Suzette had continued to make love to Raymond from beyond the grave—and how they, too, could receive passionate lovers from the Other Side.

Heather moved away from the board and began to make strange noises as she dropped to the floor and started to twitch spasmodically. When Jolene and Michaela knelt beside her to see what was wrong, Heather sat up with a leering smile and greeted them with a string of obscenities. Later, the other four girls would all swear that Heather's face was changed, altered into the features of a profane stranger.

Heather put her arms around little Joy and tried to kiss her. Jolene stepped in and pulled her away from her sister. Melanie screamed that she could see the image of a horrible, ugly woman superimposed over Heather's face and body. Michaela gasped that she, too, could see the wretched hag.

"Begone, evil demon!" Melanie shouted, holding

one of her occult charms at arm's length before her. "Begone and leave us alone!"

Heather snarled and reached out for Melanie, seizing her by the throat, seemingly intent upon strangling her.

When Darwin and Aileen Kozisek finally pushed open the door to their daughter's bedroom to see what on Earth was going on in there, Joy, Jolene, and Michaela were screaming hysterically and trying to pull Heather off Melanie.

Darwin immediately interpreted the scene as a teenager's squabble over hairstyles, boys, rock stars, or Lord knows what, so he insisted on driving Heather, Melanie, and Michaela home at once. It was when the always well-mannered and polite Heather spat in his face and swore at him in a hoarse, croaking voice that the Koziseks knew that something was very wrong.

Once again—sadly a bit late in the course of events—Jolene suggested that they all join hands and pray for Heather to return to them as she was. As Jolene began the prayer, Heather fell to her knees and began to make growling and hissing sounds. Joy screamed in horror, and Aileen carried her out of the bedroom.

A few minutes after the prayer was concluded, Heather blinked her wide hazel eyes at her friends and Darwin Kozisek, who stood ringed around her. She appeared to have no memory of the bizarre performance that had brought the slumber party experiment to a screeching halt.

Darwin changed his mind about taking Heather, Melanie, and Michaela home at two o'clock in the morning. He admitted to me that he was embarrassed about the incident and worried about what the parents of the girls would say if they were awakened in the middle of the night to be informed that unsupervised activities at the Kozisek household had driven the girls into hysterics.

When the girls arose the next morning about ten o'clock and had some breakfast, everything seemed back to normal. But after her friends had gone home, the Koziseks had a lengthy discussion with Jolene and decided to call me for advice in acquiring some preventive measures against a repetition of such an event. Little Joy had slept between her parents until morning, crying, shuddering, and lapsing into nightmares that caused her to wake up screaming. Neither Darwin nor Aileen was eager to endure a repeat performance of a teenage activity that would traumatize their twelve-year-old and transform Jolene's normally courteous friends into crude, shrieking wackos.

Establishing Protection Against Spirit Parasites

When I arrived at the Koziseks' home on Sunday evening, I was informed that twelve-year-old Joy was at a friend's house, so we could all speak frankly about the frightening occurrence on Friday evening. After only a few minutes of conversation in the Koziseks' living room, I soon determined that neither Darwin nor Aileen was aware of their daughter's experiments with out-of-body projection.

I assured them that there was nothing satanic or destructive per se in the process of astral projection, that it was really a natural thing achieved by nearly everyone at some time in their life during sleep or times of stress, but young students of metaphysics really shouldn't attempt such experiments on their own without supervision. And no one—even if an experienced teacher was present—should undergo a conscious out-of-body projection without the proper preparatory prayers of protection.

As Jolene began to feel more comfortable with me and with her parents' disapproving, but supportive, attitude toward her adventures in astral projection, she told of the dark entity that had apparently attached itself to her before she reentered her physical body.

"Such an entity is what I have come to call a spirit parasite," I said. "They may once have been humans and wish once more to occupy a physical body or they may be regarded as the classic demons who wish to invade and control a fleshly vehicle to experience human passions and emotions. Generally, these parasites of the soul cannot achieve power over humans unless they are somehow invited into the person's private space—or unless they are attracted to a human aura by that person's negativity or vulnerability. Unless you have made your prayer for protection and alerted your spirit guide, you are extremely vulnerable during a conscious out-of-body projection."

Jolene lowered her eyes and seemed to be studying my comments. "I guess I just thought that angels and guides were out there always looking after me."

"They are," I said. "But remember that there are always negative entities looking out for vulnerable humans."

I went on to say that humans are most susceptible

to spirit invasion when they are abusing alcohol or drugs and have lowered their normal boundaries of self-control. Spirit parasites, eager to experience the passions of the flesh, may enter the human vehicle at that time and encourage the possessed human to indulgence in all sorts of excesses of sex, gluttony, greed, and ego aggrandizement.

"So many beginning students of metaphysics make the mistake of assuming that their good intentions protect them when they enter trance or deep meditative states," I continued. "These individuals may find themselves particularly beset by spirit parasites because they are seeking to follow the path of Light. They present a challenge to negative entities. And when these beings from the dark side find a chink in their armor—such as inadequate spiritual preparation—they are quick to zero in on those students too impatient to take the time to pray or to surround themselves with the Light of protection."

Darwin wondered what it was that he had seen in the hallway and in Jolene's room on Wednesday night.

"Jolene told us how she felt as though another being was somehow influencing her thoughts and causing her to fantasize sexual images regarding her friends and classmates," I said. "Later, as she stared into the mirror, a kind of dual consciousness enabled her to perceive the thoughts of the spirit parasite as it admired the body in which it found itself. Still later, she saw the other face in the mirror, the face that resembled her own, yet was also reflective of the negative entity. It was that awful face that caused her to pray for the creature to leave her."

I went on to explain that Jolene's prayers had probably been quite effective in discouraging the spirit parasite from making long-range plans about inhabiting the teenager's body. If Jolene had continued to draw upon the Light, her spirit guardians would probably have been able to banish the negative entity within just a few more days. On Wednesday night, however, the spirit parasite was still able to draw energy from Jolene, and it was able to externalize itself while she slept.

"The other entity that you saw hovering near Jolene's bed," I told Darwin, "the one that seemed to be glowing, was quite likely her guardian angel or spirit guide. A spiritual balance would probably have been achieved very shortly if Jolene had not been talked into that séance. The combined energies of all those young women—especially young women open to communication with the Other Side—brought the spirit parasite renewed strength. Thank heaven, Jolene conducted that prayer circle and performed a kind of impromptu exorcism."

Darwin and Aileen asked me if I believed that the entity had left their home. I redirected the question to Jolene, asking her if she still sensed the spiritual interloper around her.

"I . . . I really don't think so," she answered after a moment of thought. "And I have been praying my knees off ever since Friday night!"

I shared the following prayer with Jolene if she should ever be aware of the return of the spirit parasite:

Beloved Angel Guide, charge me with your great strength. Charge me with your light and your love. Charge each of my vital body func-

tions with strength and energy. Keep me ever
sensitive to your guidance and your direction
and banish all evil and negativity from my
presence.

"And what about us?" Aileen Kozisek wanted to
know. "What if we should sense that evil presence
anywhere in our home?"

Fully cognizant of their concern, I told them to
practice the following simple exercise:

Bend your elbows and lift your hands, palms
outward, to the level of your chest, as if you
are making a shield of your hands. Take a comfortably deep breath; then emit the universal
sound of elevated spiritual vibration,
"oooooooom," holding the sound just as long
as you can. Repeat this until you begin to feel
the energy tingling the palms of your hands.

Once you begin to feel this energy in your
palms, visualize it as a palpable shield of love
and light that exists between you and any negative or evil force. Feel it moving around your
entire body. Image within your mind this energy of love and light feeding new power to
your entire physical being.

Utter the universal sound of "om" once again
and visualize the protective energy moving up
to the top of your head, then cascading down
in sparks of golden light, as if you were being
enveloped by a shower of heavenly radiance.

Impress upon your conscious mind that those
sparks of heavenly love represent the energy of
the Father-Mother-Creator Spirit and it descends

around your body, mind, and spirit to form a vital protective shield against all discordant and negative spirit entities.

If any of them should still sense the negative energy of a spirit parasite or any discordant entity, I advised them to visualize their spirit guardian around them moving a soft, violet, heavenly light over their physical bodies. Then say inwardly to the spirit guide:

Beloved spirit guide, angelic guardian, activate the God-spark within me and assist me in calling upon the highest of energies. Permit the heavenly Light to move around and through me. Keep this Holy Light bright around and within me and with the power of the Father-Mother-Creator Spirit banish all negative and chaotic energies from my presence.

When I left the Koziseks' residence that evening, I was assured by my careful assessment of the incident that a spiritual balance had been reinstated both in their home and in their daughter's personal province of psychic development. And I had Jolene's promise that she would not continue her experiments in any facet of the paranormal until she had undergone a process of disciplined study that would enable her more accurately to discern between the various shadowy residents of the world of the supernatural.

7

ANGELS, SPIRIT GUIDES, LIGHT BEINGS, AND SPACE BROTHERS

Leslie Smith, a writer from Pasadena, California, considers herself a "late bloomer" in the field of metaphysics. Although her deepest passion has always been to become a full-time writer, she has had jobs in many different fields, from medicine to the entertainment industry.

Then, in 1997, she lost Marie, her mother and best friend, "at sixty-two years young" from cancer.

Leslie was at a crossroads in her life. She had cared for her mother daily for nearly two years. Now her attention had to be concentrated on the sale of the family home in Staten Island before she could fulfill a much-anticipated move to California.

"It took nearly a year to sell the house," she said. "It was even more difficult selling the contents of the home—the furniture, fixtures, and thirtysome-odd years of memories. There was such a feeling of finality to it all."

The Manifestation of Spirit Lights

As soon as she had accomplished the sale of the family home, Leslie rented a house in San Gabriel, California, and began a search through prayer and healing for her true goal in life. She knew that her lifework would have something to do with writing, but the correct subject matter never materialized to allow her to set more than a few chapters down on paper before she would lose interest and want to start work on another topic.

For years, Leslie had collected various statues and artworks featuring representations of angels. These images of heavenly beings had meant so much to her mother, as well; and when she had become ill, friends and family members would always send cards and gifts with a lovely inspirational angel enclosed.

Ever since her mother's passing, Leslie had experienced a number of paranormal occurrences.

"I heard Mother crying on the day following her death—and white lights have manifested around me everywhere I have gone since then," she said. "These lights are geometrically shaped and seem to be able to take on the form of any object they choose, such as a clock, a framed picture, and then disappear. I have seen flashing light beams crisscross my walls and ceiling in the darkness of the night. In addition, there have been instances when these lights have hovered above me.

"At first I didn't know these lights were angels," Leslie admitted. "I do now."

She believes that on certain occasions in the past the angels brought deceased relatives to visit her so they could be certain that she was doing well in life. At other times, the angels were there to protect her and to guide her.

After a time, Leslie concluded that the angelic beings were telling her in thoughts and in dreams that she was to make the existence of the Heavenly Messengers known to others. Although it may have taken her a while to pick up on their wishes, once Leslie clearly understood her mission on Earth, things really began to escalate for her.

"In my dreams I was given the ideas for two books," she said. "One would feature interviews with a number of authors who had written books about angels. Another would be called *The Angel Directory*, and it would offer a complete listing of angel stories, products, and services. This book would include profiles of angel artists, musicians, and authors, as well."

God Has a Plan for Each of Us

Leslie Smith is convinced that God has a plan for each and every one of us. "Our fears block the communication," she said. "Our free will delays His mission, because we fill up our lives with so much activity that we cannot hear what is being told to us."

Upon reflection, Leslie also discovered that her mother's passing had taught her that miracles may come in many ways.

"Death can be a miracle," she said. "It doesn't have to be a devastating event, no matter how one passes from this life to the next. All we have is the present, and most of us focus on either the past or the future, thereby missing what is so crucial in the here and now."

Leslie admitted that she once feared being alone. "I always needed to fill my days with activities," she said. "I sought to work from the moment I awakened to the second I put my head upon my pillow.

"But now, I have learned much from spending time alone. I have discovered that it is in moments of solitude that we can hear what God is saying to us," Leslie concluded. "We can feel in our hearts and know what is truth. I believe that we are here to learn how to love and to share love with others."

Working in Partnership with the Light

Lori Jean Flory lives with her husband Charles in a beautiful "bit of Heaven" area of Colorado that seems custom-made for a young woman who has been communicating with angels since she was three years old. The author of *The Wisdom Teachings of Archangel Michael* [Signet Visions] and the loving, compassionate teacher of hundreds of men and women who come to her for guidance, Lori never fails to share an inspirational message that warms the heart and soul of those who may have felt frozen in their spiritual development due to the cold indifference of a harsh and careless world.

Lori always emphasizes that she is no better or any more special than anyone else, but she admits that she began to realize that she was different from others when she was three years old.

As she tells it:

Growing up, I can't recall ever being around anyone else who had the same kind of experiences that I did—nor was there anyone to explain to me what was happening to me until I was twenty-one! I don't recall that I shared a lot of my experiences with others as I was growing through childhood and my teenage years. I have been told by Spirit that the reason for this was that I might have been talked out of my angelic contact. I have always been very sensitive and intuitive in that way.

Traveling to Another Dimension at Bedtime

Daephrenocles, Lori's principal angelic guide, has told her that little spirits used to hover around her when she was three, but she said that she doesn't remember seeing them.

"I do recall that when it would be time to go to bed at night and I would put my head on the pillow and the lights were out, I would have experiences that were otherworldly," she said.

"I would hear a beautiful angelic bell, and then I would hear a frequency that would begin to rise in pitch. I would not be able to move my physical body, for that pitch would create an out-of-body experience and I would travel to another dimension. Sometimes this would happen more than once in a night.

"I never really understood these experiences as a child. During the day, I was just a regular kid, running around and playing and doing things that kids do."

As she matured, her mystical experiences began to broaden in scope, and Lori developed such gifts of the spirit as clairvoyance and clairaudience.

Her Childhood Experiences Raised Her Spiritual Vibration

In 1988, she was told that the reason for her early childhood experiences was to raise her consciousness or spiritual vibration one step at a time, so that when she was older, spirit would be able to come through her and so that she might assist, help, and uplift others.

"I never saw the angels as physical beings when I was a child," Lori said, "but I did hear and feel them around me.

"For some reason it was a long time before I had the courage to open my eyes and see what was there. I know now that we all have many helpers of love around us who are constantly guiding and helping us."

Lori is quick to protest that she does not accomplish any great things by herself: "It's not me, but the Light flowing through me. I work in partnership with the Light."

Not long ago, Lori discovered a lump in her left breast. "Naturally, I got a little worried," she said, "but I heard the angels tell me that there was no cancer.

"After the mammogram and the ultrasound, it was proven that they were right. After thirty-eight years of such guidance—I'm now forty-one—I cannot imagine life without my spiritual helpers."

Working in Partnership with the Light

Daephrenocles has told Lori that she agreed to be of service to God before her present lifetime.

"I came into this life to be a teacher of the Light," she said. "It was meant to be a part of my pathway for soul growth to radiate to others the truth that we are love and that we are here to experience love and to live love through our feelings, words, actions, and thoughts.

"I agreed to strive to fulfill a mission that would have me be on the Earth, but not of it," she continued. "I am to seek to integrate Heaven and Earth into one through the knowing that we are divine entities having a human experience, rather than being human entities seeking a spiritual experience.

"The truth is that everything we do is spiritual—even washing the supper dishes—if we do it with an attitude of love and gratitude."

As she has evolved spiritually, Lori has learned that the sacred exists in each person and that love is a mission in this life for us all.

"Each day we can imbue the special and the divine into our lives," she said. "It doesn't have to be some big, grandiose thing. Sometimes the greatest and most profound moments and truths truly come in the simple, small experiences that are of and from the heart. It is the special moments of the heart that we take with us in life."

Defining Angels and Spirit Guides
for a New Age

Although both Leslie Smith and Lori Jean Flory provide moving testimony of their interaction with beings that they identify as angels, it is likely that conservative religionists would find a great deal to quarrel with in defining the spiritual entities described by Ms. Smith and Ms. Flory as traditional "messengers of God." Those reared in more orthodox religious expressions would be likely to suggest that the manner in which these beings manifested "spirit lights," appeared in dream visions, provoked clairvoyance, and encouraged other intuitive abilities more appropriately describe the spiritualist medium's spirit guide than heavenly angels. And Christian fundamentalists would probably insist that these ladies might be in touch with *something* on the Other Side, but that it couldn't be those glorious winged beings in heaven who sing God's praises throughout eternity.

So what is the difference between a spirit guide and an angel?

Strictly speaking—and drawing upon ancient texts from the Bible to the Qur'an—the angels are a species apart from us humans. And in the traditions of Christianity, Judaism, and Islam, an angel is directed to a human by the Supreme Being for the purpose of delivering a message of guidance, offering spiritual counsel, or in some extreme instances, providing the miraculous healing of a physical illness or accomplishing a rescue from threatening circumstances.

If we adhere to the traditional definition of an angel, we humans do not die and become angels.

We are a separate creation from our cosmic cousins, fashioned a "little lower" and of material substance, rather than assembled of ethereal vibrations of light.

For centuries now our popular culture has perpetuated the myth that people become angels when they die. We've all shed a tear along with James Stewart when his daughter hears the ringing of the bell on the Christmas tree in the final scene of *It's a Wonderful Life* and recites the oft-repeated folk wisdom that the chiming of such a bell signals another angel receiving its wings. "Atta boy, Clarence," Stewart winks knowingly, and we, the audience, are in on the secret that the awkward angel Clarence, once a human, has earned his wings and advanced a rank in the angelic hierarchy.

A proper definition of "spirit guide" requires us to draw from many different spiritual traditions.

When spirit mediums speak of their guide, they are referring to the entity from the Other Side who assists them in establishing contact with deceased humans. The spirit guides of mediums usually claim to have lived as humans on Earth before the time of their physical death and their graduation to higher realms of being.

In many shamanic traditions, the spirit guide serves as an ambassador from the world of spirits to the world of humans and often manifests to the shaman to serve as a chaperon during visits to other dimensions of reality. It seems quite likely that today's mediums and channels are contemporary expressions of ancient shamanic traditions.

Native American traditionalists and others who follow the old teachings go on vision quests to learn the identity of their spirit guide and their symbolic totem animal manifestation. These men and women trust that their guides are concerned about them and observe their earthly activities.

While mediums and many shamanic traditions believe spirit guides may be summoned during altered states of consciousness, orthodox religious traditions insist that angelic missions originate from a higher power and therefore lie beyond a human's desire to initiate contact. One may pray *for* angelic intervention, but one must never pray *to* an angel. A consistent dogma in all traditions warns against worshipping either angels or spirit guides.

According to these delineations, we may be making some progress toward drawing a distinction between spirit guides and angels. But when we speak of the concept of a *guardian* angel, the boundaries that are supposed to separate the two categories of ethereal entities truly become blurred. Guardian angels and spirit guides are both nonphysical, multidimensional beings whose mission it is to provide important guidance, direction, and protection for their human wards on the physical plane. Nearly all traditions assign the guardian angel or guide to watch over their human from the time of the soul's birth into the physical Earth body until the soul quits its corporeal shell for the Other Side.

Thus it is that so many contemporary spiritual seekers began to wonder if the differences between a spirit guide and a guardian angel are not largely a matter of semantics. As New Age thought began to spread, more and more such seekers preferred avoiding issues of religious, shamanic, or spiritualist dogma and began to refer to any benevolent, compassionate, otherworldly entity as a Light Being.

But when the UFO contactees came on the scene in the 1950s and began to channel messages from the Space Brothers, clear-cut distinctions between angels, guides, Light Beings, and the new missionaries from Outer Space once again became rather murky.

Angels and Spirit Guides in Spacesuits

In 1963, when I first began seriously investigating the claims of the UFO contactees, those men and women who proclaimed that they were in contact with beautiful, benevolent beings who piloted the flying saucers arriving on Earth from other physical worlds in the universe, I drew immediate parallels between those who channeled Outer Space beings and the spirit mediums who provided inspirational messages from their guides. After I had listened to a good number of sermons relayed by the contactees from the "Orthons," the "Zumahs," and the "Mokas" from Venus and beyond, my background as a psychical researcher saw how similar these messages were from the inspirational words communicated by spirit mediums from the "Katie Kings," the "Shooting Stars," and the "Professor Gillespes" from the Other Side and beyond.

And when many of the contactees told me that the UFOnaut had appeared to them in a "light and vaporous form" because of the different frequencies between our dimensions, I was again reminded of the "light and vaporous forms" that had long been associated with the séance room and the spirit circle.

By 1966, I had distilled the following elements from the Outer Space Gospel of the UFO contactees:

- Humans are not alone in the solar system. They have "Space Brothers," and they have come to Earth to assist humans to become better and more spiritual beings.
- The Space Brothers are here to teach, to help awaken the spirit within all humans, and to help them rise to higher levels of vibration so that the human species will be ready to enter new dimensions of being. Such a goal was precisely what Jesus, Buddha, Mohammed, Confucius, the prophets of old, and the leaders of the great Earth religions have tried to teach those humans who would listen.
- The entire human species now stands in the transitional period before the dawn of a New Age. With peace, love, understanding, and brotherhood, humans will see a great new era beginning to dawn.
- If the people of Earth should not raise their spiritual vibratory rate within a set period of time, severe earth changes and major cataclysms will take place. Such disasters will not necessarily end the world, but shall serve as cataclysmic crucibles to burn off the dross of unreceptive humanity. Those who die in such dreadful purgings will be allowed to reincarnate on higher levels of development so that their salvation will be more readily accomplished.

As one who has also studied carefully the spiritual teachings claimed by those who have received contact with angelic beings as well as those who have received inspirational lessons from spirit guides, I can easily substitute "angels" or "spirit guides" in every one of the above tenets of the Space Brothers' Cosmic Gospel. In my opinion, the phenomenon of the Space Brothers has absolutely nothing to do with the question of whether extraterrestrial intelligence has visited Earth. In my assessment, the Space Brothers are the familiar supernatural entities—angels, guides, Light Beings, call them what you will—hiding themselves in more contemporary, and thereby to some humans more acceptable, personae.

For many years early in my research I wondered if such entities and the information they relayed might originate in the channeler's or medium's own Higher Self, rather than from any distinct and separate external intelligence. And of course, I had always the opinions of skeptical and cynical colleagues who insisted that all appearances of angels, guides, or benevolent outer space beings are the manifestations of self-delusion, externalized projections of the revelator's own personality.

I have wrestled with the knowledge that psychologists hold it as an axiom that whatever the conscious mind represses, the unconscious embodies in allegorical form, either in dreams or in conscious creative imagery. Demons, for instance, often serve as personifications of undesirable emotions, such as lust and hate. The manifestations of angelic beings could be simply the externalization of deep spiritual feelings that are increasingly denied expression in our secular, technological, materialistic society.

But my fifty-year study of the "Other," my nearly thirty-five-year analysis of the *Steiger Questionnaire of*

Mystical, Paranormal, and UFO Experiences with its thousands of inspirational testimonies of human lives altered by some supernatural intelligence, and of course, my own personal mystical experiences with my spirit teacher and various spirit beings have increasingly convinced me of the reality of an external intelligence that has interacted with our species since our creation on this planet. I do believe that, throughout history, these beings have sought to communicate certain basic physical and spiritual truths to *Homo sapiens.* I am also convinced that some kind of symbiotic relationship exists between us and this intelligence. In some way, they need us as much as we need them, for we are both part of a larger community of intelligences, a complex hierarchy of powers and principalities.

So call these beings by whatever name seems most appropriate to you, but test the motives of whoever manifests to you by cautious discernment. Both the positive and the negative entities will quite likely appear in whatever form is most immediately acceptable to you on your level of spiritual acceptance.

Brenda Montgomery of Morro Bay, California, enjoys a fine reputation as a healer, as well as a nationally recognized channel for higher spiritual intelligences. Herewith she shares some proven techniques for establishing contact with one's spirit guide.

"Your Spirit Guide Is There for Your Highest Good"

Brenda has been hearing the spirit voices for many years. As a child entering the first grade of elementary school, however, she didn't realize that the voices she heard were actually those of her guides from the higher dimensions.

"As I look back," Brenda recalled, "I thought these voices were my 'dream friends.' And even as a child, I talked to the voices as if I had known them for many, many years; and I wondered why they didn't come to talk to me every night, only at certain times."

As closely as she can remember, the voices came into her awareness in the silence of the night, and she could hear them in her head. "I did answer them out loud," Brenda said, "but softly, so that my parents would not hear me. Even at that young age I knew at some level that this was not something that they would understand."

In the years to come, Brenda began to channel spirit voices as a part of her metaphysical work. "There were many different voices that came to me," she said, "and all of them were those beings who were my spirit guides and teachers. There were some female voices among them, but most spoke in male voices and they were all great teachers. I totally accepted their wonderful words of love and information.

"Thus began many, many years of work for me, which became a wonderful and pleasing aspect of my mission. To this day, friends and strangers still write to me and ask questions for my spirit guides to answer. To do so is one of my most creative and blessed moments in life. My mission in life is to listen to the guidance of these spirit teachers and share their wisdom with others."

The Importance of a Prayer for Protection

Before Brenda begins the process of receiving contact from her ethereal teachers, she always prays a prayer of protection. "I ask God to protect me and all who are with me from any spirit that does not wish us well," she explained. "I ask only for those spirit guides who come for our highest good. I have never had any 'evil' spirit come to me. But this is the point! You must always ask only for those beings who are of the Light and who are there for your highest good.

"If you do not do this," Brenda emphasized, "any entity can—and will—come just to say whatever it wishes to say—and then you are in trouble! There are lots of spirits out there who just want a human voice to speak through and who do not care for our highest good. Much harm can be brought to you if you do not bring in the Light and ask for God's help in this matter of receiving guidance from your spirit teacher."

Brenda went on to say that it is always a *must* to pray first, and then to ask for the highest and best guides available. Asking for the White Light around the room and around yourself is also a *must*.

"No matter how safe you *think* you are," she stressed the point, "there are entities on the Other Side that will see you as nothing more than a way to enter the Earth realm. They do not care at all what happens to you.

"Always protect yourself with the White Light! When you do this, those who come to speak will be the highest and the best, the ones who have words of wisdom and beauty to speak to you.

"Sit for a while in meditation," she advised, "and when you are totally relaxed, ask for your guidance to come. You will be surprised how much information you will receive if you open yourself to hear. Please don't be disappointed if you don't actually *hear* a voice in your ear, but be open to all the ideas that flow through your mind and be prepared to write them down so you don't forget them. In times of crisis there is so much peace in speaking to your guidance for a moment. They are always there to help us."

Here are Brenda Montgomery's techniques for connecting with your spirit guides:

1. Sit down in a quiet place at a time when you can be totally alone. Take the telephone off the hook or put the answering machine on very low. Put a note on the front door that you cannot be disturbed for an hour or so.

Select a comfortable chair in which you may sit for thirty minutes to an hour. Have a pen and paper next to the chair. You might need a blanket to help you to feel warm and safe, so just cuddle up with your feet flat on the floor and your hands in your lap.

Take some rather deep breaths and allow yourself to begin to relax.

When you begin to feel very relaxed and kind of sleepy, ask God or the White Light to be with you. Ask for protection throughout your entire meditation. Ask and *believe* that you are fully protected. When you have faith in the Light of God, then you are on your way.

2. After you have sat still for a while, feeling totally safe in your blanket, surrounded by the protection of the Highest Ones, silently ask for your spirit guide to come to you. Ask for only one, and the guide from whom you need to hear will come. (They can't all come at once, for we each have many guides and teachers.) Spirit usually comes as Light in the beginning, but if you are especially open to this process, you may become aware of the actual appearance of your own personal guide or teacher. Do not be afraid, for you are protected by the White Light.

3. Now is the time to ask your spirit guide the questions that you need to have answered. Don't try to ask about all the things that you have always wanted to know. Begin with only one or two questions, and ask only one question at a time. You will need to write down all the information that you *hear* or *sense* at the moment it comes through. To do so will not disturb your meditative state. Simply close your eyes after you are finished writing the answer to the first question and begin to ask the next one. If you are truly in a state of belief about your ability to hear your spirit guide, you can keep on for an hour or so, asking and receiving answers to all that you need to know.

But know this: your spirit guide needs to be held

in the highest esteem—and you need to regard this information as blessed. The more you believe in this wonderful process, the more information you will receive.

In addition to being a nationally recognized channel for spirit intelligences, Brenda Montgomery is an accomplished artist and photographer. "I believe there is something about the creative process that attracts spirit energy," she said. "Always welcome those beings who come in the Light to give you the blessing of spiritual help. My life has been a stream of wonderful guidance, and I thank God for that gift."

8

WE ARE SPIRITUAL BEINGS EXPERIENCING MANY DIMENSIONS

When she was six years old, Kathleen Curry contracted double pneumonia, a bad situation that was made worse because she had a heart condition that made her susceptible to diseases. Both of her lungs filled with fluid, and she was running a very high fever.

Her family lived in a rural area, and by the time her father and grandmother rushed her to the hospital an hour and a half away, Kathleen's lungs had collapsed. Although she was not expected to survive until morning, during that night of crisis the little girl underwent a near-death experience that demonstrated to her that angelic help was available to her and that she would never be alone.

This is how Kathleen described the experience:

I remember floating above my body and seeing a figure in front of me that was neither male nor female, but was made up of thousands

121

of golden sparks of light. The figure identified itself to me as my guardian angel, and a kind of instinct, a knowing within me, understood this to be true.

The angel explained telepathically that I had to return to my body because it would make my parents very sad if I died then. The angel also said that it was not yet my time and that I had much to do with my life. I was not anxious to return to pain and suffering, but I was reassured that I would be watched over and cared for by not one, but many angels. I remember reentering my body through my head and feeling searing pain in my lungs. The angel touched me and stayed with me for a while before it disappeared.

Today Kathleen Curry is a college instructor and professional symphony bassist who lives in New York. Although she did not speak of the encounter with her guardian angel during her near-death experience until years later, she indicated in her return of the *Steiger Questionnaire* that she had seen the angelic being and felt its presence many times since her decision to return to an earthly existence.

Kathleen said that she has been saved from wild beasts, poisonous creatures, and evil people who intended to hurt or kill her. "While driving, I have been prodded when I've fallen asleep," she said. "Once in a bad rainstorm, I was trying to find my aunt and uncle's house. I got off on a flooded road, and I cried aloud for help. The next thing I remember is driving into my aunt and uncle's driveway. Only *seconds* before, I had been *miles* away!"

In every instance, Kathleen stated firmly, "I give thanks for the help and the appearance of angels, who have often remained invisible or taken other forms to assist me."

Kathleen holds the opinion that "God and God's messengers interact in one's everyday life." Because she was provided with the knowledge, wisdom, and certainty of an afterlife at a very early age, she feels that she has a responsibility to tell people the comforting message that they all possess a spiritual body and that their true home exists in another dimension.

"We are all born with the knowledge of our spiritual nature," she said, "but we have a veil of forgetfulness put over us which we must strive to pierce while we are alive. We are all spiritual beings and can experience many dimensions. What we choose to do on Earth is our choice, but to deny, ridicule, deter, or prevent that message from reaching others will retard our own spiritual growth. Likewise, to set up false goals, such as wealth and materialism, will make this world an even more evil and tough place in which to live."

It has been given to Kathleen to understand that we are responsible for each other and for the Earth.

"The whole point of our taking earthly bodies is to know and act upon this," she said. "Each day should be lived with that in mind— to help others as well as yourself in any way you can. To be indifferent to the needs of others makes us responsible for poverty, greed, and suffering."

Kathleen also wishes to advise the unsuspecting that there exist darkside angels, who try to retard the spiritual growth of humans. Such dark entities are attracted by the negative thoughts and actions of men and women who give their energy to other than spiritual goals.

"If we avoid fear and anger, which retard our progress and frustrate our goals, then we will eventually succeed," Kathleen commented.

Kathleen seeks to fulfill her obligation to the angelic ministry through singing and by playing many musical instruments. Her creative expression is designed to praise God and God's helpers.

"We must always seek to assist others," she said. "There is never any need or excuse for arrogance. We picked our circumstances ahead of time to help others as well as ourselves. So I sing, pray, and yell from the depths of my soul, 'Praise God! Thank You for this adventure!'"

She Keeps her "Spiritual Antenna" Fully Extended

Although Bridget Martin has an associate degree in electronic engineering, she found work in "for-profit" corporate environments to be unfulfilling. She has chosen to turn her back on high-salaried jobs and prefers to work for nonprofit organizations. She currently serves as a church secretary in Cincinnati.

"I want in some small way to give to my Creator, since He has given so much to me," she explained.

Bridget developed an interest in spirituality at a very young age. Her mother remembers that even before her little daughter could read and fully understand the loving, divine nature of Jesus and his mission to Earth, Bridget would thumb through the family Bible and kiss his picture.

Then, when she was nine, Bridget had the "eye-opening" experience of witnessing the spirit of an elderly man floating toward her.

Reflecting back on the incident, she said, "Of course I was extremely frightened, but the spirit was harmless."

Asking God for Wisdom

Coupled with her growing interest in spirituality was Bridget's desire to attend church. At that particular time, her parents did not attend any church services, but her mother granted her wishes by taking her to a nearby place of worship.

It was here that the girl learned about a life-changing experience that the minister called "salvation," and when Bridget was ten, she asked God to come into her heart.

"Not long after my life-changing experience, I asked God for wisdom," Bridget said. "At first I was scared to do this, because I had read, 'He that increaseth wisdom increaseth sorrow,' but I knew that I wanted it. I felt this request would enable me to help others.

"When God felt I was ready, He began to open my eyes to new knowledge. As I had feared, these revelations did not always come without tears or pain."

Experiencing Prophetic Dreams and Visions

Bridget began to experience prophetic dreams and visions, such as the ones in which she escorted the souls of children into Heaven. She would enter the rooms where children lay dying, comfort them, and accompany them to a higher world. As they traveled through space, she could feel the wind on her face and experience vivid colors.

It was also at this time that Bridget had begun to study religions other than Christianity and learn valuable spiritual lessons from them as well. When she told a friend who practiced Hinduism about her heavenly dreams, he expressed his opinion that she was experiencing "transcendental flight."

A Light in the Sky That Spawned Tornadoes

When Bridget was fourteen, she dreamed repeatedly about an intense light in the sky that grew and spawned tornadoes.

She was afraid the dream was about to come true when one day she looked up at the sky and saw a bright light other than the sun. Her mother laughed when Bridget told her that many tornadoes would come soon.

"Later that day," Bridget said, "Mother was surprised when tornadoes ravaged Xenia, Ohio."

The "Good Samaritan" Who Disappeared

Bridget has also experienced the dramatic intervention of an angelic being.

"One rainy morning, I was driving to work on a busy expressway when a car swerved into my lane," she recalled. "I applied the brake to keep from hitting the intruder. When I did so, my vehicle skidded out of control. A pickup truck hit my vehicle as I slid toward the median.

"When the 'demolition' was over, I saw the front of the truck. It was distorted, and broken glass was scattered on the blacktop."

Bridget's first fear was that the driver of the truck might have been killed. Remarkably, she could get out of her own battered vehicle.

She ran to the truck and saw that the driver, a young man, was not seriously injured.

As she stood in the road, trying to pull herself together, a middle-aged good Samaritan said to her, "I saw the accident. I stopped the traffic so that you and the other driver would not be hit again."

The man pointed to his white car, which signaled the other drivers to slow down.

Bridget immediately walked toward the truck driver and commented, "Wasn't it nice of that man to stop and help us like that? He risked his own vehicle and his safety to help us."

The young man looked confused and asked her, "What man?"

"I whirled around and saw that the good Samaritan had vanished," Bridget said. "Where his car had been just moments before, a police car with flashing lights now warned motorists of the accident scene."

Bridget is convinced that a guardian angel was there on the highway that day and that God had prevented a fatality. "The middle-aged 'man's' face was pleasant and his smile reassuring," she said. "I thought later about the white car and remembered the Bible's association with the color white and purity."

Bridget Martin said that she is thankful to God— or the Great Spirit, as her Native American ancestors called Him—for all the help that He has given her and her loved ones.

I have told Him that my spiritual 'antenna' is fully extended, so that I may receive all the messages that He is willing to give me," she said.

A Most Unusual Otherworldly Visitor

Freddie D. O'Malley has spent the last fifteen years of his life in the field of law enforcement and is currently senior correctional officer with the U.S. Federal Bureau of Prisons at El Reno, Oklahoma. A thoughtful, serious man, O'Malley has reflected for long hours concerning the great importance of discovering his fellow humans without fear, ego, or personal agenda.

"I want always to be able to pause for a moment and be thankful for the company of others with honesty and respect for their individualism," he said. "I want to be able to see past the differences between people and focus solely on the humanity and the Oneness we all share."

Freddie has experienced many paranormal and metaphysical incidents in his life. "Some were only simple observations of unusual phenomena," he said.

"Others include out-of-body experiences, lucid dreaming, and even encounters with odd 'visitors.' I have also experienced a number of events that were more spiritual in nature, sublime and pleasant."

A Strange Kind of Script Covers the Sky

Just months after his father's death in the summer of 1967, four-year-old Freddie O'Malley had an encounter with an otherworldly visitor.

"I was playing in the sandbox with the family dog when I noticed the entire sky was covered with some kind of strange script," he recalled. "This writing had the appearance of covering the entire sky from horizon to horizon. The characters or letters were dark gray or black, giving the impression of a giant newspaper folded over the summer sky that had previously been very fair."

Freddie shouted for his mother, who came out of the house, and he asked her to read what it said in the "giant newspaper" that covered the sky.

"She was unable to see the strange script that, to me, was so obviously there," Freddie said. "I became very frustrated, but she insisted there was nothing in the sky. Moments later the 'newspaper' was gone, and the sky was normal."

A Glowing Ball of "Fuzzy Light" Manifests Before Him

But the boy's mystical adventures that afternoon were not yet over. Later, there appeared before him a glowing ball of fuzzy light about the size of a basketball.

The object came to rest a few feet above the ground and about ten feet in front of Freddie. Then, to his astonishment, the center of the ball of light unfolded and revealed what appeared to be a very small person at the end of a tunnel of light.

According to Freddie:

The light was intense, but it didn't hurt my eyes to look at the whole incredible scene of a being of light that moved closer to me and grew larger and larger.

At last the Light Being stood before me—very tall, radiating swirls of white-hot light with blended rays of yellow and blue dancing around its body. The Being was solid, yet made of light.

I wasn't afraid or threatened, but felt excited. I had the impression, but only intuitively, that the Being was female. It also expressed itself in a gentle and graceful demeanor.

The Being began to speak or make a declaration, but I could hear nothing at all. I shouted at it to speak louder, so I could hear—but there was still no sound, only an occasional glance my way and a gentle smile every now and then.

Freddie called for his next-door neighbor, who was like a grandfather to him. "I asked him to help me understand what the angel was saying. Soon his wife and my mother came outside to see what was going on."

Freddie remembered being confused and upset that the people he trusted the most were of no help. "How could they not see this magnificent being, so beautiful and amazing?" he wondered.

After a short time, Freddie said, the Light Being shrank in size as it moved back into the "tunnel" within the luminous ball of light. As it moved into the distance, the ball of light collapsed inward on itself, sealing up the tunnel and returning in shape to a uniform, spherical orb of fuzzy white light. The object then rapidly departed, quickly disappearing in the summer sky.

"From that time on, even as a child," Freddie said, "I knew that I had a purpose in life that I must accomplish."

A Childhood Experience Led to a Lifetime Study of the Paranormal

Quite understandably after such a childhood experience, one of the principal emphases in Freddie's life is the study of the paranormal and spirituality.

"This is something I must do," he said. "I encourage others with mystical experiences of their own to talk freely and share their stories. Some are afraid to talk out of a fear that they'll be ridiculed, so they opt to keep everything bottled up inside of them.

"I tell people that it is okay to talk about these

experiences," he continued. "It isn't always manda-
tory that they understand what happened to them—
and never do I claim to have all the answers—but I
encourage people not to bottle up their feelings but
to speak freely of their paranormal and mystical
encounters."

9

A RAGGED STRANGER RESET HIS MORAL COMPASS

It certainly seemed during those early years that Timothy Guy of Tarzana, California, was doing everything right in preparation for leading a righteous existence. He experienced twelve years of Roman Catholic schooling and earned a college degree. Because he had always been on the spiritual side, he even spent time in a seminary contemplating entering the priesthood.

However, instead of serving God in the pulpit, he decided to serve a very different kind of congregation—and he joined a rock band.

"This was during the seventies," Tim, author of a recently published book, *Aliens Over America,* acknowledged, "a time when many of us were living under the Hippie Bill of Rights—free sex, drugs, and rock 'n' roll—all of which seemed to go hand in hand."

But still a spirituality burned inside him. He quit the band to pursue a more contemplative life, but soon discovered that the immediate result of such a decision was no income.

He Questioned Whether Life Had Any Meaning

At the same time, other aspects of his life began collapsing before his eyes. It seemed as though his decision to seek the Spirit had afforded him no discernable rewards. Rather, everything appeared to have been taken away from him.

If this was how God treated his friends and those who sought his guidance, Tim mused, no wonder He had so many enemies.

He continued to pray, but he heard no answers. He grew despondent and became angry with the Eternal. He began to wonder if life had any meaning at all.

After a year of prayer and no response, Tim decided that he had had enough.

"Fuming at the thought of feeling duped, I packed my worldly possessions in my VW bug and headed up to Yosemite National Park," he said.

"I was prepared to backpack into the high Sierras and challenge God to show His hand. If God is not here for us in life, will there be a God after death? Why wait to find out?"

He Encounters a Ragged, Mangled, Bedraggled Being

The following evening, as he was about to light his campfire and begin cooking supper in a lonely

Yosemite campground, Tim Guy encountered a most unusual being—who appeared from out of nowhere, riding a bicycle.

"He looked terribly mangled—a crippled ankle, a paralyzed arm, and a hole in his throat where his vocal cords should be," Tim said. "He needed the hole to breathe."

Ad then an extremely weird thought occurred to Tim: "Actually, his whole demeanor looked a lot like me. I, too, was a frightening sight on the inside. (Later, I came to learn that the entity was perhaps what is known as a doppelgänger, one's spiritual double.)"

The peculiar intruder to his campsite definitely had Tim's attention as he leaned his bicycle against the VW bug and began to walk toward him. When they looked eye-to-eye, Tim felt guilty for the suicidal thoughts that had been afflicting him.

The ragged stranger motioned toward Tim's canteen for a drink of water, and after he had taken a few swallows, he poured the rest of the water over his sweaty head. Tim was startled to see only patches of hair on the man's head, as if his skull had been cracked open and then surgically repaired.

In their ensuing "conversation," standing face-to-face with Tim, the strange being never said a word. "But he communicated via a booklet of symbols that he wore on a chain around his neck," Tim recalled. "He would point to the symbols, and somehow I was able to decipher his replies."

Tim asked the stranger how he had gotten there. He replied that he had been in a coma and still might be.

"I asked him if he saw God," Tim said. "He relayed to me that he felt God's presence, that it was

All-Encompassing, and it may seem that we plead to the Presence to be released from our pain and receive no release, but this isn't true. The Spirit is our Breath, and therefore cannot help but respond. It's just that all too often we do not have the eyes and ears—the wisdom—to appreciate this.

"God Is and God is good. I, Timothy Guy, was a soul worth singing about, and I should know this. Otherwise, he foresaw for me a gloomy doom."

Tim asked him what he was supposed to do. "He didn't have symbols for that."

The Stranger Disappears, But Leaves Tim with a Valuable Insight

The following morning, when Tim awoke alongside his car in his sleeping bag, he found himself alone. He had, however, awakened in a very different state of mine. He didn't remember the being departing, but he must have fallen asleep immediately after their conversation without even lighting the campfire.

In Tim's words:

> I awoke, and in a flash of God-given insight, I recalled that God Is and God is good. This insight, like all double-edged swords, has proven to be both a blessing and a curse. It's a blessing that I can never knowingly stray without alarms going off in my head. My moral compass is pretty strong. And it's a curse in that I can never get angry and question God's existence again. God Is and God is good.

Today, it is my full intention to know that when I die and stand naked before the Maker, and his Awareness wants to know how my soul was occupied on the physical plane, we shall both know what it was spent in earnest pursuit of the Source. Until then, like all spiritual warriors, I must trod through the uncertainty of life.

Encountering a "Genuine Hindu Sikh"

Timothy Guy adds an interesting footnote to his story. Exactly one year after his encounter with the angel in Yosemite, he discovered that a "genuine Hindu Sikh," with high turban and long white beard, was living in the house next door to his.

The holy man was eighty years old at that time, and Tim was delighted to learn that his landlady had given the Sikh permission to use the pool during his early-morning ritual. Once a week thereafter, for the next fifteen years, until the holy man died at the age of ninety-four, Tim sat at his feet and learned from him.

"When I asked him how I came to meet him," Tim said, "he replied, 'You found me in your own reflection.' "

The Sikh refused to teach Tim how to meditate in the Hindu manner.

"He said that it would take forever for a Westerner like myself to achieve enlightenment in this way," Tim explained. "Our minds have become bombarded with too many images, images that have become embedded and must be resurfaced. Freedom of speech has its drawbacks to the serious scholar of God."

The holy man suggested that Tim find a mantra, a God phrase, and do a physical exercise with it. While he might find his mind wandering in and out of fantasies, his mantra would always help to anchor him back to his God phrase.

Tim Shares His Personal Mantra

Here is Tim's personal mantra, which he performs to a series of five breaths:

(Inhaling) "Bless" (Exhaling) "me" (Inhaling) "Fa—" (Exhaling) "ther." (Inhaling) "I" (Exhaling) "am" (Inhaling) "your" (Exhaling) "son." (Inhaling) "Ah—" (Exhaling) "men."

Do this throughout your exercise, and you will find that the mantra will carry over into your underbreath as you go about your daily routine. You will find that your mind chants the phrase without your conscious effort. Once the mantra is in the undercurrent of your breath, you will have a greater chance of retaining a God-consciousness throughout the day. I believe this process is more effective than meditating Eastern-style for twenty minutes, then rising up to face the bombardments of the Western world.

An Irreplaceable Gift from God

Tim considers his relationship with the Sikh holy man to have been an irreplaceable gift from God.

"He was my guru—although he always insisted, 'No, *you* are the guru'—and I was his disciple," Tim recalled. "He will remain in my prayers until the day I die. Spirituality is an atmosphere. *Sat Nam.*"

The holy man's final advice to Tim lay in these words: *"Beyond our understanding is God's mercy."*

Tim also remarked that his guru left him with one legacy: the gift of tears.

> His words rearranged my soul in such way that I cry almost daily now. Not out of sadness or pain, but at anything that expresses the Joy of Being—like children, laughing or otherwise, or the sight of a bag lady. Watching cheering sports fans on television with the sound on "mute" will also bring out the tears in me. It's a gift.

One Saturday night while Tim was taking a late-evening stroll, he poked his head in a local bar and heard a good sixties rock 'n' roll band.

"I stepped inside, bought a beer, and somewhere during that set, a conga line formed to a Beatles song," Tim said. "And when the front girl congaed up to me, she motioned to me to turn around, and so I did. She placed her hands upon my waist, and I led the weaving dancers behind me in and among the tables, taking on more dancers with every table we passed.

"As destiny would have it, that was the night my

guru died," Tim continued, "and there I was, beer in hand and leading a conga line in some down-and-out beer bar in Tarzana. Fortunately, a friend of mine later pointed out that I was, perhaps, leading the wake. And I'm Irish, so that works for me."

Perceiving the Unseen Hand Behind All Miracles

When people question Tim's belief in an Eternal God, he replies that he can only give them his perceptions of how he now perceives the Unseen Hand behind even the smallest of miracles.

"I wish that I had a book like the one that the strange being in Yosemite brought with him, a book of symbols to point to explain things to people," Tim said. "But you cannot pass on faith like a baton in a relay race."

Although Tim says that he feels blessed and in a state of God-consciousness, physically, he admits, he still stubs his toe. "Mentally, I can tie myself up with pretzel logic," he conceded, "and spiritually, although my moral compass is strong, the currents of life can still flow me off-course. I do believe in reincarnation and karma. We reap what we sow.

"Since we live a quick journey through a brief mystery, I believe one should always think positively," Tim said. "For me, that translates into a belief in a Power higher than ourselves."

10

THE SEERESS WHO TALKS TO SPIRITS

It was about 1973 when I first met an attractive blond writer and actress named Clarisa Bernhardt who was becoming very diligent in the exercise of her paranormal abilities. In a very short time of ascent, Clarisa has risen to become one of the most well-known psychic sensitives in the world.

Through the years, Clarisa has become a dear friend to both my wife Sherry and myself, and she is always eager to share details of her special techniques for contacting the spirit entities and higher intelligences that she says comprise our greater Cosmic Family.

"I have always felt that I am to use my intuition or psychic abilities to try always to be of assistance to others and, hopefully, to prevent potentially tragic events," Clarisa said.

Because so many of her predictions have proven to be accurate, there have been those critics who have questioned whether or not Clarisa could be interfering with Fate.

"My answer is that if I have been given information about a future disaster, then there is a hope that it can be prevented—and I feel that I must do my best to help," she explained.

Since Childhood, Clarisa Has Been Aware of Other Dimensions

From her earliest childhood memories, Clarisa has been aware of otherworldly things.

"I could see beautiful lights—auras—around most people," she recalled. "And then I realized that I could also see into dimensions other than our own. I also perceived that there was a definite difference between these dimensions. Very early in my life it appeared that my life would be centered around otherworldly explorations."

Later, as an adult, Clarisa began to study more seriously spiritual and metaphysical teachings.

"One of the marvelous lessons I learned was the principle that 'we are ever becoming,' that we are evolving and growing as much as possible in this lifetime," she said.

"Many lifetimes down this path we will eventually be beyond any negative influences such as jealousy, hatred, greed, envy, and so forth, and be capable only of becoming love.

"And when I speak of love," she explained, "I am not referring to a personal love or the state of being 'in' love, but I refer to an impersonal love that will lift you above time and space—a love that comes from the spirit within."

An Exercise to Banish Negative Thinking

To help achieve a mental attitude receptive toward such harmony, Clarisa suggested the following exercise:

> Sit quietly. Breathing through the nose, take three deep breaths and hold each breath as long as it is comfortable to do so . . . then exhale slowly.
>
> Clear your mind of all thoughts, and think of yourself as a light in a darkened room.
>
> Image a gold light completely surrounding yourself, a light which has become one with you.

Clarisa recommends this simple exercise whenever you feel negative emotions—such as jealousy, envy, or hate—seeking to affect you. Practiced daily, this technique can help to balance those negative emotions which may attempt to manifest through you.

We Must All Learn to Be Careful of Our Thoughts

"We must be very careful of the thoughts we allow to accompany us," Clarisa advised. "As if to emphasize the importance of this exercise, on a recent early summer morning I was awakened by the sound of an inner ethereal voice which clearly said, *"Dispel darkness with love so that the Light can enter."*

In the vision that followed these words, Clarisa

saw a cloudlike force of pink energy, symbolizing love, that was moving toward a dark energy field of equal size.

"The pink force literally pushed the dark energy from view," she said. "Then there was a magnificent light of unequaled brilliance. I was delighted by this vision, and immediately used the information received to harmonize a condition which had been challenging me."

Predicting Earthquakes and Communicating with the Space Brothers

For many years now, Clarisa has considered herself blessed to receive communications from numerous and varied members of what she calls the "Cosmic Family." Some of her contacts have been with celestial beings; others have been with entities who have identified themselves to her as "Space Brothers."

It was these benevolent beings who contacted her after her first public prediction of an earthquake on Thanksgiving Day, 1974.

"The earthquake had occurred exactly as I had forecast it on my radio show *Exploration* (KRVE radio), including the date, the location, the magnitude, and the exact time to the minute," Clarisa said. "My purpose in making the prediction that I had received from a vision was to demonstrate that psychic abilities were real."

And then, after the prediction had come to pass, according to Clarisa:

The Space Brothers teleported me to their spacecraft and informed me that they had "repaired" me so I might receive information from them more clearly. They explained that they can transcend time and space and raise their vibratory rate to a frequency wherein they just move from one space-time continuum to another.

They also confirmed that some future quake predictions which I had made following the Thanksgiving quake were indeed going to occur. They advised me that the quakes that I had predicted would be the two largest quakes in 1975, which proved to be true.

Since that initial encounter, the Space Brothers have transported my consciousness to their spacecraft while my body was resting on my bed. On other occasions when I lived in California, they appeared to me in the garden area outside my home. They have even teleported me after I have parked my car on a trip to the grocery store.

A Chilling Vision of Red Riding Hood Shooting President Ford

On August 5, 1975, as Clarisa walked through the state capitol grounds in Sacramento, California, she had a sudden, chilling vision of Little Red Riding Hood aiming a pistol at President Gerald Ford. In the vision, Clarisa saw clearly the consequences of the assassination attempt if it were not stopped.

"I immediately gave this information to a contact of mine with the FBI," she said. "He asked me if I knew when this attempt on Ford's life would take place, for according to the FBI bulletins, they had no information that the President was planning to visit California anytime soon. My vision had 'told' that what I had seen would occur in exactly one month, on September 5th."

It is now a matter of record that on September 5, 1975, Lynette "Squeaky" Fromme, a member of the Charles Manson Family of social misfits, approached President Gerald Ford while he was in Sacramento with the full intention of assassinating him. She was wearing a bright red hood, thus making her easy for the FBI and the Secret Service to spot and to halt before she could pull the trigger.

"The FBI expressed great interest in my source for providing such detailed and accurate information," Clarisa said. "I tried to explain to them that I was only the messenger, only delivering information."

On two other occasions, when she quietly managed to avoid the media, Clarisa was able to assist in preventing assassination attempts on U.S. Presidents.

The Space Brothers Warn of Sabotage to NORAD

In March 1979, the Space Brothers provided Clarisa with information about a serious sabotage attempt which was being planned for NORAD in Colorado. Clarisa immediately sent a Western Union Night Letter to the U.S. State Department in Washington, D.C., advising them of the potential danger of the sabotage attempt.

"The following November 1979, an incident took place which many chose to credit to a technological error when someone 'accidentally' placed a computer test tape, programmed with simulated attack scenarios, into the *real* early-warning computer," Clarisa said. "According to United Press International, the error was undetected for six minutes while nuclear-armed B-52s actually prepared for takeoff in response to the 'nuclear attack.' "

Thankfully, Clarisa declares, the "accident" was detected.

"My purpose was to deliver the warning to NORAD in an effort to avoid a tragedy," she said. "While NORAD officially held to the story that it was due. to 'the accidental loading of a wrong tape,' off the record they admitted to me that there was the possibility that it might not have been an accident at all, but an act of sabotage."

Angels Kept Her Airliner Aloft

It would take an entire book to do justice to Clarisa Bernhardt's incredibly accurate predictions regarding earthquakes and national and international events. She also utilizes her contact with angelic beings in situations that are much more up close and personal.

For instance, in November 1998, she was flying from Kansas City to her home in Winnipeg. Shortly after takeoff, the pilot announced that a massive snowstorm was heading in their direction, and they would be entering turbulent weather. Everyone was advised to fasten their seat belts and to expect to keep them on throughout the flight.

Clarisa took additional precautionary measures:

When it really started getting bumpy, I closed my eyes and employed an exercise that I had used before to contact the angels. Suddenly, on the screen of my mind, it was as if I was outside the airplane, observing it as it flew. Then I directed my thoughts to the angels.

I asked them to please harmonize the weather. I visualized an angel in front of the plane with the nose of the aircraft resting on its shoulders. Then I imagined an angel for each wing and another to support the plane's tail section. Almost immediately the bumpy flight became smooth.

After about an hour of a smooth flight, I could see huge storm clouds ahead of us—so I visualized twelve additional angels dressed in robes of electric blues, bright pinks, emerald greens, and brilliant golds. Next I pictured them moving the dark clouds and clearing a path for our airplane.

I can tell you that we enjoyed an incredibly smooth, nonforecasted flight.

Even as we descended through the clouds, there was not one bump. The pilot commented over the loudspeaker what an unexpectedly smooth flight it had been.

A Technique by Which You May Link Up with the Angels

As an important facet of her mission of endeavoring to prevent disasters and striving always to assist people in their personal lives, Clarisa shared this exercise by which you might establish your own linkup with the angels:

"One early morning, as I was awakening, three angels told me that they sincerely want to be of help to others," Clarisa said. "However, a person must specifically ask for their assistance. Here is a way that I understand that you may receive help from an angel:

> Just as you are preparing to go to sleep, recall in your thoughts that the angels definitely wish to help you—but you must ask them.
> In their communication to me, there were three angels, so in your mind's eye, visualize three angels standing before you.
> Be very comfortable with their appearance and mentally, telepathically, tell them that you are aware of them and that you appreciate their offer of assistance. Respectfully request that they listen to you, then state your request or concern.
> After you have done this, thank them for any help they can give you—and then release the thought and go to sleep.

Clarisa stressed that it is very important for you to clear your mind of all thoughts after you have made your request.

"Go to sleep knowing that if it is possible for the angels to help you in this particular situation, you may be assured that they will," she concluded. "It's all really very simple. Don't feel uncomfortable about asking the angels for help. I'm sharing exactly what was told to me by the angels, and I've seen this work on many occasions."

11

HE COLLABORATED WITH AN INTERDIMENSIONAL BEING AND BECAME A PIONEER OF NEW AGE MUSIC

Ever since I was a very small child, I have from time to time heard the most beautiful music swirling around me. For instance, when I would sit in my personal sacred place amid the lilac bushes, I would hear lovely, enchanting music emanating from the very leaves and branches.

The celestial music still plays for me almost nightly. I have, in fact, become spoiled over the years, and I find it difficult to fall asleep until I hear either the heavenly orchestra or the soothing voices that often manifest in its place.

I love music. As the wise sage Confucius observed, music expresses the harmony of the universe, while rituals express the order of the universe:

> Through harmony all things are influenced, and through order all things have a proper place. Music rises to heaven, while rituals are patterned on Earth . . . Music . . . correlates with

Heaven and creates rituals to correlate with the Earth. When rituals and music are well established, we have Heaven and Earth functioning in perfect order. [*Book of Ritual*, 19]

For me, listening to music is a total experience that completely sweeps me away into other worlds, other times, other dimensions. And recent research indicates that music may elevate our brains as well as our moods.

Although the July 2000 issue of *Harvard Men's Health Watch* admits that it is not yet clear how music appears to improve spatial reasoning and other cognitive functions, "researchers speculate that listening to music may organize the firing of the nerve cells in the right half of the cerebral cortex, the part of the brain responsible for spacial functioning. According to this construct, music—or at least some forms of music—acts as an 'exercise' that warms up selected brain cells, allowing them to process information more efficiently."

All right. That means I can listen to music and warm up certain brain cells for more efficient mental performance, but I am still dismayed that I have never been able to express myself creatively through music. It has always troubled me that I seem to have absolutely no musical talent of any measurable degree at all. Why am I not able to recreate the wonderful celestial music that I hear by means of some musical instrument or by the creative act of composition?

I asked the question of my good friend Iasos, a brilliant musician who heads his own Inter-Dimensional Music company and who has created such masterworks as *Angelic Music, Elixir, Jeweled Space, Timeless*

Sound, and *Sacred Sonic Tools.* In 1975, Iasos, along with his colleague Steven Halpern, another good friend of ours, pioneered and began what came to be known as "New Age Music."

Iasos, generous friend that he is, argued that he fully believed that I could sit down and create beautiful music if I *really* wanted to—but wasn't writing all those books and articles enough creative expression for me?

A College Student Begins to Hear "Unusual Music" in His Mind

Iasos's family moved to the United States from Greece in 1951 when he was four. He began taking piano lessons when he was eight and flute lessons when he was ten, but by the time he went to college at Cornell University, he found that he preferred pursuing his musical studies on his own, analyzing music from many different cultures.

"Then, around 1968, I began spontaneously and surprisingly to hear music in my mind, as if I were wearing headphones," he said. "This was a *most* unusual music.

"Emotionally, it felt much more heavenly and loving than normal earthly music. And it also included many unusual sounds not at all typical of earthly musical instruments. Since this was before the era of electronic musical synthesizers, I had no frame of reference at all for these unusual sounds."

After graduating from Cornell in 1968 with a degree in anthropology, Iasos decided to move to California to dedicate his life to manifesting for others the "heavenly music" that he heard in his mind.

"I didn't think *everyone* would like it," he admitted, "but I believed that many on the planet would love it—and that they would find it as uplifting, healing, spiritually invigorating, and harmonizing as I did. But then my logical mind would kick in and say, 'You don't even have the foggiest idea of how to create sounds like those, much less the music itself!'

"Then to my amazement, I heard a voice inside my mind—very male, very powerful, and with infinite conviction—say to me, *'You can do this!'* "

Iasos Meets Vista, His Transmitter of Musical Visions

In 1972, Iasos had a profound experience wherein, while doing automatic writing, he made contact with a unique personality and experienced a kind of "flash-memory-recognition."

Although the "flash" may have lasted only one second in linear time, after the extraordinary experience Iasos *knew* beyond any doubt what his life's mission was to be. Since that moment, Iasos affirms that he has steered forward, solidly and clearly, never wavering for even an instant from the mission that had been revealed to him by a being named Vista.

According to Iasos:

All this time, Vista had been intentionally transmitting all these musical visions into my mind. Vista was the being with whom I had made a preincarnation agreement that we would work together while I was incarnated.

In that instant flash of memory, I knew that I dearly loved Vista, the way a younger brother looks up to and adores an older brother. Our agreement was that he was to transmit musical visions into my mind so that I could manifest them and make them available to all who would be responsive to such music.

Creating Interdimensional Music to Raise Awareness

Iasos explained that the whole point of interdimensional music was not to gain "fame and fortune" for its performers, but to create music that would help men and women to make the leap into higher vibratory rates as our entire planet continues to raise all its frequencies to higher and higher realms.

To more completely explain the purpose behind his agreement with the being Vista, Iasos said that their spiritual collaboration was to create and make available:

1. Music that can help Souls achieve an enhanced resonance-connection with the grander part of who they are.
2. Music that can function as a vibrational gateway into celestial dimensions of Light and Love and Awareness.
3. Music that can facilitate body energies fine-tuning themselves into a higher and more refined resonant coherency.

4. Music that can help bridge the connection and merging with one's Light Body.
5. Music that can directly nourish the Soul through a continuous stream of concentrated beauty patterns.

Although he was imbued with the creative energy to produce this interdimensional music, Iasos had to face a material reality. He had almost no money. And if he continued to work with other musicians to pay the bills, he knew that he would be stuck making "normal earthly music," instead of the nonearthly celestial kind.

"Through sheer willpower and chutzpah, I eventually succeeded in convincing some patrons to help me buy my first four-track tape recorder, so I could begin creating my own multitrack music creations," Iasos said. "I knew that I could not afford to have other musicians working with me, but once I had a multitrack recorder, I could play all the musical parts one at a time on tape, then play all the parts together simultaneously to create the final sound.

"I was so happy when I left the music store with the recorder in my hands. My heart was pounding with excitement, and I thought to myself, 'Now that I have this four-track recorder, *nothing can stop me!*' "

Maintaining a Working Relationship with an Interdimensional Being

In the years since Vista first made his identity known to him, Iasos has maintained a connection with the interdimensional being.

"When a musical vision is transmitted to me, I simultaneously receive three things," Iasos said. "First, what the music is to be, that is, the chords, melodies, composition, and so forth.

"Second, how to create that music, such as technical tips on how to create special sound effects or sounds for that particular piece of music.

"Third, what effects that musical composition will have on those people who respond to it. And Vista's readout on these effects is always perfectly accurate."

Iasos emphasizes that the manner in which he works with Vista is not trance channeling. "I am *always* in a normal conscious state when I'm working with him," he said.

"Perhaps it is more accurate to say that is an overlapping of our consciousnesses which allows musical ideas to get transferred. Another way of looking at this would be to say that Vista 'superimposes' certain artistic ideas over my consciousness. I then experience those ideas as artistic inspiration.

"Since Vista and I think alike when it comes to beauty-in-sound," Iasos continued, "this makes it easy for him to influence my artistic choices when I am working on a piece of music. So the distinctions between was it Vista's idea or was it my idea become blurred and quite irrelevant."

Experiencing Vista in a More Tangible Way

Iasos recalled the time in 1976 when he was backstage waiting to perform a concert at a church in Redwood City, California, and he began musing that it would really be nice if he could experience Vista in a more tangible way than he usually did.

"I telepathically put out the following request: 'Dear Vista, I would *really* like to feel and sense your energies right now in a much more vivid and tangible way than I normally do,' " Iasos said. "About a second and a half later, I suddenly had this immensely *intense* rush of energy zapping into my third eye. *Brrrrt!* And it was over, but it had packed an almost incomprehensible amount of visual information into that tiny blip of transmission."

Here follows Iasos's attempt to explain what was transmitted to him in that very brief "blip":

Today our civilization has an incredible amount of visual effects—video visual effects, film visual effects, optical visual effects, computer graphics visual effects, and so on. Most of us have seen videos that are a continuously changing parade of glorious visual effects. Well, imagine watching about thirty hours of the most gloriously beautiful visual effects you can conceive of, with each effect transforming into the next style of effect and each effect becoming even more glorious than the former. Imagine all these effects emanating outward from a center point and continuing outward until they leave your field of vision as yet-newer patterns emerge from the center point and flow outward. Imagine watching a continuous thirty hours of this! And then imagine compressing these thirty hours of gloriously beautiful visual effects into a one-third section of a "blip" that zaps like a

spark into your third eye. Thirty hours com-
press into a third of second!

Iasos states that it has taken him years to contemplate, absorb, process, assimilate, and think about the
visual effects that Vista bestowed upon him in that
brief "zap" in 1976.

"Others have said that one of the attributes of a
being of higher consciousness is the ability to pack a
lot of information into a tiny package," Iasos said.
"And this third of a second 'zap' is the most potent
application of this concept that I have ever personally
experienced."

At the time that he received the transmission, Iasos
had no idea how to implement or to create such effects. Then, years later, the *how* manifested in kalei-
doscopic projectors, special lighting effects, computer
graphics, and so forth.

A Request to Channel Words Is Denied

In the early 1980s, when the channeling of multidimensional beings became something of a New Age
fad, Iasos admitted that he began to feel a little
jealous.

"Here all these various channels were bringing
through these fascinating and exciting bits of information, and all I was receiving was music. So I decided
to ask Vista if he would channel some words . . .
thoughts . . . ideas . . . concepts to me."

The answer Iasos received was totally unexpected.
Vista responded with a comical posture of indigna-

tion and disdain: "What? You want us to drop down to the level of mere *words*?"

"The implied, unspoken thought was clear to me," Iasos said. "Vista was in effect saying, 'Here I am giving you these glorious transmission of radiant, highly concentrated, multisensory Beauty Patterns—as sounds, visuals, and feelings—and you want me to drop down from this to communicate in the highly limited conceptual methodology of linear thought-symbols!' "

Iasos couldn't keep from laughing at Vista's posture of disdain, but he got the message: their agreement was to create concentrated Beauty Patterns, and he was going to stick to their initial understanding.

According to Iasos's understanding, human emotions vibrate on unique frequencies, with the so-called negative emotions, such as fear, anger, jealousy, and rage being lower frequencies.

"Although my basic nature is to be happy, even perky, on those occasions when I am vibrating with depression—a slower, lower vibration—I am totally incapable of receiving any input whatsoever from Vista," he explained. "Regardless of what he may be trying to transmit to me, my lower vibrations of depression will block my reception. That is why I try always to cruise on my usual higher vibration of happiness."

Iasos knows that Vista always and fully honors his free will.

"This even includes the possibility that I might at any time decide to no longer work with him," he said. "Vista has never interacted with me to keep me on course—although I am certain that he wishes me to do so.

"Such beings as Vista have something called 'infinite patience'—a quality I suspect is easier to attain when one is functioning outside the realms of time and space."

The Process of Transmitting a Musical Vision

If Vista always and fully honors Iasos's free will, how does the being prompt the musician to produce a particular piece of music that he wishes to be created?

"He seduces me into creating it!" Iasos declared. "To attain his goal, while simultaneously honoring my free will, he transmits a musical vision into my mind that is so beautiful, so endearing, so awesome, so overwhelmingly divine that it melts my heart.

"Once I have entered that surrendered state of a totally melted heart, I acquiesce. I say to Vista, 'Yes, I do commit to manifesting this music—no matter what! I *will* manifest it!' And so far, I have always kept my promise, no matter what was happening in my personal life."

Iasos explained that his "normal" manner of composing on the piano is to follow the "emotional path" of a piece.

"Each chord is a unique emotion," he said, "so a sequence of chords is a sequence of emotions—or an 'emotional path.' So I just tune in to my heart, get in touch with the emotions that I'm feeling, and then 'translate' those emotions into chords. I continue this process, appending the feelings that flow out from the last-created feelings, until the whole piece is composed. And as I translate these feelings into chords, I write down these chords as they become clear to me so I do not forget the sequence of chords that I am freshly creating."

Crystal's "Tiny Bubbles of Light"

As the years of collaboration with Vista have progressed, Iasos has also met Crystal, the interdimensional being's feminine counterpart or partner.

"Whereas Vista is always all business and totally concentrates on sending me these glorious musical visions, Crystal feels free to assist me in a more flexible, less-structured manner. She sends me emotional support in the form of a unique energy which is a specialty of hers. This energy, called 'Liquid Crystalline Essence,' is available to all those who call on her—three times in a row, according to cosmic protocol—and request her to transmit this marvelous energy to them."

Iasos describes Crystal's showers of Liquid Crystalline Essence as feeling effervescent: "Like champagne or ginger ale! It sparkles in a manner that makes you feel very light and exhilarated. Imagine millions of tiny bubbles of Light, all exploding with the happy desire to raise your vibratory rate. However, unlike liquid, this energy totally passes *through* you, filling the mostly empty spaces between all the electrons of your being."

Iasos greatly enjoys feeling the loving and caring energy of Crystal around him. "To be honest, I'm actually very turned on by her," he admitted. "And she expresses her affection by showering me with Liquid Crystalline Essence, which always leaves me light-headed, exhilarated, and often with an uncontrollable grin on my face. To have such an immensely evolved being sending me her personal loving radiations feels just sublime."

"Follow Your Joy and Excitement!"

When I asked Iasos what advice he might give to those who have not yet committed themselves to accomplishing a particular mission here on Earth, he responded with his usual enthusiasm: "The best way for anyone to discover his or her unique purpose in life is to learn to follow their joy, to follow their excitement."

Explaining further, Iasos said:

Your excitement is caused by a resonance with your Higher Self. Excitement is a sign that the activity you are contemplating is aligned with your Higher Self, and this alignment is what causes the excitement. When you are aligned with your Higher Self, it turns up the life force within you, and you experience this acceleration as excitement. So, by simply following your excitement, you are using that excitement as a compass-heading from your Higher Self to guide you in the direction that your Higher Self wants you to go—the direction of your life's purpose or mission.

This does not mean that you need to make some profound all-encompassing decision like,

"What is the most exciting thing that I can do in this life?"

No, all this means is that in each Now-Moment, you ask yourself, "Of all the things that I could actually do *right now*, which one of those things is the *most exciting option*?" And then whichever option seems most exciting to you, go for it.

Iasos believes that the process of continuously and consistently following one's excitement will naturally lead an individual to do what he or she is meant to be doing:

"What your Soul *hopes*, your earthly free will chooses to do. When you are *excited*, you are aligned with your Soul, you are aligned with your Higher Self, you are aligned with your purpose in life, you are aligned with your mission in life."

He concedes that there is a "tricky part" to this process:

"What if your excitement suggests doing something seemingly unrelated to anything that could be your life's purpose?" he asked by way of illustration.

"For example, what if your highest, most exciting option at the moment is to go to a diner and get some french fries? *Follow your excitement even then!* Because that seemingly trivial event might just lead you to meet someone who could further you in your life's mission.

"*So stay on target, even when the target seems trivial,*"Iasos insists. "Follow your excitement even when it may seem not at all related to anything like your mission in life. Your Higher Self *knows* when it's steering you, because it has a much vaster perspective of things than you do here on the physical dimension."

According to Iasos, when you follow your excitement and do what excites you, this means:

1. This activity is *you* and it is truly aligned with your Soul.
2. Because it is *you*, this activity is *effortless* for you.
3. Because it is *you*, the universe will *support* you—including financial support—to continue accomplishing your mission in progressively more expanding ways.

Remember, Iasos advises, regardless of whether you wish to become an innovator of music, literature, or business, make a practice every few hours or so to ask yourself, "Of all the things that I could actually do *right now*, which one of those things is the *most exciting* option? And then go for it!"

12

FINDING YOUR SACRED PLACE AND RECEIVING DREAM TEACHINGS

I cringe when I hear someone say that a profound teaching message received in a dream was not real. It was just a dream.

Just a dream, indeed! Dreams have altered the lives of individuals and changed the course of nations.

Everything that humankind has ever created began with a dream, an image in the mind, an inspiration. We humans make nothing *real* that did not first have its seed in the mind. If it were not for dreams, visions, and inspirations, humankind would still be cowering in dank caves and begging for fire from a lightning storm to keep back the nameless dread of darkness.

One of the most asked questions that I have received from readers and listeners over the past thirty years has been, "How may I receive dream teachings from my spirit teacher or guide?"

In order to address such requests as completely as possible, I have decided to make this chapter an instructional one, filled with general advice and specific exercises designed to encourage the reception of dream teachings.

I, like so many others, began receiving dream teachings when I was a child. I have utilized these nocturnal instructions to write books and structure my life. Those dreams, visions, and inspirations that I have received on my earthwalk are among the truly *real* blessings that I have experienced. And I have loved the challenge of transmuting their energy into material-plane manifestations of books, articles, and seminar programs.

You may have heard it said in certain metaphysical circles that you can create your own reality.

More correctly, I believe, that which you really create is your basic *attitude* toward reality and how to choose to deal with it in every aspect of your existence.

One of the most important tools for individuals on their mission in life is the learning of effective fantasy play in order to enable them to face all of life's crises in a confident and creative manner. From time to time I am chided by those who feel that I am careless in suggesting that we are playing a Reality Game. Life, they remonstrate, is a serious business. One does not "play" at it.

However, I believe that when we are truly able to apprehend the full significance of the eternal contest that we knowingly or unknowingly play with the powers and principalities, seen or unseen, that share our universe, we will thereby attain such control of our life and our abilities that we will be able to confront all aspects of existence with the same ease and freedom with which we enter a game with friends.

In his *Myths to Live By*, Joseph Campbell describes a very special manner of polite, aristocratic Japanese speech known as *asobase kotoba*, "play language." In this convention, one would *not* say to another, "I see that you have arrived in Tokyo." Rather, one would state, "I see that you are *playing* at being in Tokyo."

Campbell goes on to inform us that the idea behind *asobase kotoba* is that the person addressed is considered to be in such control of his life and his powers that for him everything is play, a game. He is able to enter into the flow of existence as one would enter into a game, freely and with ease. Those duties which must be performed are attacked with such a will that in the performance, one is literally at play.

In my opinion, a very important step in approaching life as creative play is to learn that every event may be dealt with from several perspectives. The particular perspective which you select as your individual reality construct must not only be *believed in* by you— you *must become it*.

And one of the most effective means of achieving this kind of confidence in dealing with your perspective of reality and the successful accomplishment of your mission is to open yourselves to receive dream teachings.

Identifying Your Personal Sacred Place and Moment

Before I present some exercises to prompt your psyche to connect with a higher source that will provide you with your own dream teachings, I want you to take a few minutes to identify your own personal sacred place and moment.

Those scholars who study such subjects as anthropology, mythology, and religion have theorized that all of our various ritual observances have their genesis in a faraway beginning time, a sacred event to which a particular culture can trace its origin. A familiar illustration for those of us in the Judeo-Christian tradition would be the story of Adam and Eve and the Tree of Knowledge. For at least three thousand years, we have traced the creation of our humanity, our species consciousness, and our world to that symbolic event.

Each of us has our own personal myth of "the beginning" of a special kind of consciousness regarding the external, material world around us.

Each of us has a memory of a special time to which we might return in our own individual sacred moment and our unique ritualized measurement of reality.

I can remember being a small boy as young as two or three and crawling into the midst of a clump of lilac bushes, where I sought refuge from the demands of physical reality. From this magical spot, I was able to perceive the world from my own special vantage point.

I can remember that whenever it seemed as though the confusions and the frustrations of the outside reality—the one that I shared consensually with my parents and others—became too much for my budding psyche to comprehend, I could retreat into my sacred space in the lilac bushes and take some time to process just exactly how best to deal with the present stressful challenges.

Even now, as an adult in my sixties, whenever I feel that the consensual reality that I share with family, friends, and colleagues becomes a bit too much for me to handle, I return in my memory to my special, magical place—my own mythical moment of the advent of my consciousness as an individual spiritual entity in a very strange material world.

Whenever I need a sturdy fortress and a temporary respite from the stresses and pressures of external reality, I mentally return to my sacred place in the lilac bushes. It is from this eternally safe and secure vantage spot that I am able to regroup my energies, recharge my psyche, and resume my mission with renewed strength.

I know that each of you has a similar magical, mythical place—perhaps it was in your closet or under the dining room table—a sacred spot to which you retreated as a child and felt secure and protected against the fears and awful awareness of a reality external to you and to your inner spark of divinity. In learning to utilize your dreams to receive important spiritual teachings, first practice lying in bed and remembering your individual sacred place before you fall asleep.

Remember the magical place with all of your senses.

With the memory of your sight—recall every detail of your mythical spot's appearance.

With the memory of your sense of smell—remember any odors that associated with your secret spot.

With the memory of your sense of hearing—think back if there were any particular sounds that you heard when you retreated to your special place.

With the memory of your sense of taste—remember if there were any tastes connected with this place.

Once you have reviewed all the sensory details of your sacred place, then you are ready to pull in the power of your internal myth and use it to help summon the dream teachings that you most need to assist you in a successful fulfillment of your mission.

Preparing to Receive Dream Teachings

Dream teachings, visions of guidance, and inspirations are all best achieved by entering sleep time or periods of meditation with the proper goals held foremost in your mind. To help me achieve a receptive mindset, I very often remember the words of Grandmother Twylah, the wise shaman who initiated me into the Wolf Clan Medicine Lodge of the Seneca:

It is in the forest that the ancient ones recognized the presence of *Swen-i-o*, the Great Mystery. The force of the Great Mystery penetrated into every soul, making every soul a part of it. When alone with their thoughts, the ancient ones listened and *heard* the Silence of the Great Mystery. They listened and *saw* the Silence. They listened and *tasted* the Silence. They closed their eyes and *felt* the Silence deep within.

The woodlands became their chapel and their bodies, their altar. In the Silence they communicated with their Creator, and they received peace and spiritual teachings.

As I recall Grandmother's words, I visualize myself approaching a quiet, sacred place in a forest to begin my journey into the Silence. On occasion, I see myself kneeling on a blanket next to a small waterfall, closing my eyes, and allowing myself to enter the Silence of deep meditation.

According to the cosmology of the Seneca, the holiest energies are concentrated in the Silence. The essence of the Silence is Light and Love, and pulsating deep within this luminous energy is the Great Mystery, the Source-of-All-That-Is, God. It is when one enters the Silence with an attitude of reverence and respect that one is receptive to the most powerful dream or vision teachings.

Feel the Sacred Energy of the Silence Enter Your Spiritual Essence

Prior to your seeking a dream teaching, sit or lie quietly and concentrate on feeling the energy of the Silence touch you.

Feel the energy focus on your spiritual center (visualized for mental assistance as your Crown Chakra, the top of your head) and in your physical center (visualized for mental assistance as your Heart Chakra, the center of your chest).

Take three comfortably deep breaths and *know* that the sacred energy of the Silence has permeated the spiritual and physical centers of your own essence.

Be still—within and without—and know that the power of the Silence has entered all levels of your consciousness and all levels of your being.

Take three more comfortably deep breaths, holding

each for the count of three. Feel at one with the essence of the Silence that has blended with you.

Now visualize a bright, golden glow emanating from your Heart Chakra and your Crown Chakra. In your mind, imagine two rays of golden light traveling from your Heart Chakra and your Crown Chakra to your personal concept of a Supreme Being, the Great Mystery, the Source-of-All-That-Is.

See those rays of golden light from your Heart Chakra and your Crown Chakra traveling to the very Heart of the Universe. As the connection is made between your Heart Chakra, your Crown Chakra, and the Source, see points of violet light emanating from every part of your body.

Concentrate for a moment on making your body as still as possible. Direct your attention to the Source, the great Mystery, and focus upon the rays of golden light that emanate from your Heart Chakra and your Crown Chakra.

See clearly the rays of light that you are transmitting to the Source.

Feel your consciousness melding with Higher Consciousness and visualize yourself holding open hands to the Source, as if in supplication.

Now begin to request a dream teaching from the Highest Source-of-All-That-Is.

Mentally affirm the following (or create your own variation in keeping with the essence of the following supplication):

> O Great Mystery (or whatever term for the Supreme Being you may prefer), grant to me a dream teaching that will inspire me with strength, energy, and great creative power.

Grant that the dream teaching I receive will show me those things that I need to know for my good and my gaining and the accomplishment of worthy tasks on Earth.

Visualize the Source, the Great Mystery, as the eternally powerful energy that creates the golden glow emanating from Your Heart Chakra and your Crown Chakra.

The more clearly, the more profoundly you can visualize this connection, the greater the results of your prayer for a dream teaching.

Expanding Your Consciousness Prior to Receiving Dream Teachings

Here is an excellent technique that will help you to expand your consciousness just before falling sleep and receiving dream teachings.

Visualize a pool of water before you.

Visualize the pool wherever you would most wish it to be—perhaps in a forest or at the foot of a majestic mountain or in your own backyard.

See yourself tossing a pebble into the pool and allow your *consciousness* to become *one* with the ripples that spread across the pool.

See the ripples of your consciousness moving farther and farther across the surface of the pool.

And now visualize your consciousness rippling from the center of the pool toward the farthest horizon, moving, moving onward, until your ripples have touched the farthest horizon and turned back to form a great circle.

You are in the center of this great circle, continuing to send forth ripples of consciousness.

You are in the center of a great circular pool of cosmic energy, and your ripples are now touching all the farthest points of the horizon—east, west, north, south.

You are now aware of yourself only as a *focal point* in the midst of the great pool of Time, the great pool of *Creative Energy*.

Open your heart and spirit to the blessings that will continue to return from the ripples that circle back from each horizon. Let your spiritual essence linger in the great pool of Creative Energy.

Receive ripple after ripple of greater consciousness returning to the very center of your awareness as you permit yourself to fall asleep to receive profound dream teachings that will enrich your life to earth.

Programming Your Dreams to Receive Teachings

It is possible to program your dreams in the sense that you can rehearse the appearance of various symbols to manifest in your dreams and you can prepare your dream persona to recognize them as signaling the advent of dream teachings.

As I said in a previous chapter, one of the most basic mechanisms for the receiving of visionary experiences and higher awareness, such as those received in dream teachings, is the development of a mental construct of a spirit teacher who will provide you with important insights in dealing with your day-to-day trials and tribulations, as well as your goals of higher awareness. As I explained, you may visualize this wise spirit teacher translating guidance from your own Higher Self or you may believe that you are truly making productive contact with an actual spirit teacher in your dreams, visions, or creative visualizations. And remember, you may visualize your spirit teacher as either male or female, whichever gender you wish.

Visiting the Crystal City of Dreams with Your Spirit Teacher

Unless you have some other method of relaxing yourself and allowing your consciousness to enter a light altered state, use the relaxation technique provided in Chapter 5, "Meeting Your Spirit Teacher."

Once again I remind you that it is possible for you to read the relaxation technique and the visualization process, pausing now and then to permit their effectiveness to permeate your mental/spiritual essence. If you choose to explore these techniques on your own, without the assistance of another, remember to pause frequently to ponder the significance of your inner journey and to allow your awareness to be elevated to a higher spiritual realm.

If you feel that you may receive greater benefit by becoming more of a receiver than a transmitter of the exercise, try reading the relaxation technique and the visualization process to a like-minded friend or family member, permitting that individual to accomplish spiritual contact and dream teachings for his or her own betterment. Then, later on, that same friend or family member may assist you in reaching a state of deep relaxation and allowing you to achieve your own spiritual linkup to receive dream teachings.

It is also quite possible to record your voice reading these techniques into a tape recorder, so that you might play the tape back and allow your own voice to guide you through the relaxation process and through the heavenly realm.

Any of these methods can be effective. Your success in achieving the highest value to your mission will depend upon your willingness to permit such an experience to manifest fully in your consciousness.

Take three comfortably deep breaths and proceed with the complete relaxation technique provided in Chapter 5.

The Process

Once the subject is completely relaxed, continue with the following process:

Your body is relaxed, but your mind—your True Self—is very aware.

Now a beautiful golden globe of light is moving toward you. You are not afraid, for you realize—you *know*—that within this golden globe of light is your spirit teacher, one who has always loved you. You have been aware of this loving, guiding presence ever since you were a child, a very small child.

You feel love moving all around you as you see manifesting before you now the face, form, structure, and stature of your spirit teacher. Feel the love that flows to you from the very presence of your spirit mentor.

You remember the name of your spirit teacher. Speak that name *now.*

Now your spirit teacher is stretching forth a loving hand to you. Take that hand in yours.

Know and understand that your spirit teacher is about to take you to the dimension of spirit where important teachings await you. You know that you are about to move into a higher vibration of reality.

You know that you will travel with your spirit teacher to the *Crystal City of Dreams,* where you will receive very important teachings for the physical and spiritual enrichment of your life on Earth.

Now, hand in hand, you feel your spirit teacher, lifting you higher and higher.

As your consciousness blends and flows with that of your spirit teacher, you see that the two of you are moving toward a mystical place of higher vibration. You are moving toward a sacred place of higher awareness, of higher consciousness.

At the count of three, you will be in the *Crystal City of Dreams* with your spirit teacher.

One . . . rising higher and higher.

Two . . . higher and higher, almost there.

Three . . . you have now arrived in that heavenly place of wisdom for which your spirit has always yearned.

Look around you. The trees, the grass, the sky— *everything* is more alive here. The colors are more vivid.

Look at yourself. You, too, have been transformed. It is as if you have a new, more finely tuned, nervous system.

You have new eyes to see those things that you have never before seen.

You have new ears to hear what you have never before heard.

Look at the beings who have come to greet you. Feel the love emanating toward you from their eyes and their smiles.

Many faces seem very familiar to you. It is as if you remember them from another time, another place.

Some reach out to touch you, to embrace you. Feel the love flowing all around you.

As you follow your spirit teacher through the *Crystal City of Dreams*, you feel love all around you, and your spirit teacher tells you that you may come here to this place of love, wisdom, and knowledge whenever you wish.

You now stand with your spirit teacher before a beautiful golden temple, a temple of love, wisdom, and knowledge.

It is in here, your spirit teacher tells you, that you are about to perceive a particular symbol that will appear in your dreams whenever you are to be given a teaching.

This symbol will be something personally significant to you.

You will know it as soon as you see it and recognize its deeper meaning to you.

Remember, whenever you see this symbol in any of your dreams, you will know that it heralds an important dream teaching.

You will clearly see this symbol at the count of three.

One . . . you see the symbol beginning to form.

Two . . . the symbol is becoming much clearer.

Three . . . you see the symbol clearly and fully and completely understand it. Remember it always. This is your personal symbol that heralds important dream teachings.

You may now ask your beloved spirit teacher any question that you wish that pertains to the successful reception of dream teachings. You may also ask for the solution to a personal problem that is troubling you.

Your spirit teacher may answer in words, in a series of gestures, or by presenting you with another symbol.

Watch closely and listen, for your spirit teacher will answer your question at the count of three.

One . . . watch and listen!

Two . . . the answer is coming.

Three . . . you see or hear and understand it *now*!

[Pause here for about thirty seconds to permit the spiritual teaching to be received.

If the answer to more than one question is desired, the above instructions may be repeated.

If a dialogue is established between the subject and the spirit teacher, permit it to continue as longs it is productive.

When the contact begins to fade or when the desired information is received, begin to bring the subject back to full consciousness in the following way:]

Now you must return to full consciousness in the physical realm of Earth.

Do not sorrow. Know and understand that you may return to the *Crystal City of Dreams* again and again, as often as you wish. You are never separated from your spirit teacher on the spiritual vibration.

At the count of five, you will be returned to full consciousness.

One . . . coming awake.

Two . . . coming awake and remembering the symbol that will herald your dream teachings.

Three . . . coming more and more awake, feeling very good in mind, body, and spirit.

Four . . . coming awake filled with the knowledge of your dream teachings.

Five . . . wide awake and feeling great! Filled with love and greater awareness!

Receiving a Gift of Awareness from a Spiritual Master

This creative visualization allows the subject to receive a teaching of spiritual enlightenment and awareness from a spiritual master. Once again, the spiritual master may be visualized as either male or female, but I will use the masculine pronoun to avoid the awkwardness of the "s/he" construction or repeating the "his or her" duality with each reference to the ancient wise one.

If a deep state of relaxation is desired in order to increase a greater state of receptivity, use the complete relaxation technique described in Chapter 5.

Excellent results may also be achieved by allowing the subject a few moments to relax the physical body and to focus mental alertness by taking three comfortably deep breaths.

The Process

See yourself walking up a mountain trail under the light of a full moon. The trail is easy to see in the moonlight, and you have no fear of falling.

You see that you are approaching an ashram, a spiritual retreat, wherein dwells a very honorable, very old, and very wise Spiritual Master.

You know and understand that you have been invited to appear before the Master and to ask him [or her, whichever gender you wish] a question regarding your receiving vision and dream teachings. You are pleased that you have been granted an audience with this wise teacher.

Take a moment now to experience fully your emotions as you walk up the mountain trail.

Feel deeply any expectations that you might have.

Look around at the environment of the Master. What plants grow near the trail?

What is there about the mountains that most captures your attention?

As you approach nearer the retreat, what do you most notice about the houses and outlying buildings?

Now you turn off the mountain trail and begin to walk up the path that leads to the front gate of the ashram.

Be aware of all things near the path. Be aware of your inner thoughts and feelings.

As you stand before the gate, a student in a dark robe appears and opens it for you.

Thank the student for the courtesy and continue into the ashram.

Now you are able to see the dancing flames of a great open fire burning in the center of a courtyard. You are able to see someone dressed in robes sitting near the fire.

You know that it is the wise Spiritual Master.

As you look toward the Spiritual Master, become

totally aware of him. See his clothes, his body, his face, his eyes, his mouth.

He gestures to you to be seated. See the way he moves his hands.

A student appears and hands you a cup of the Master's favorite tea.

Take the cup. Lift it up to your lips.

Taste the tea in your mouth. Savor it. It is a special tea, exceedingly flavorful, a bit spicy, yet mild, gentle to the palate. Remember its unusual taste and flavor.

The Spiritual Master nods to you, indicating that you may now ask a question about how you may best acquire meaningful dream teachings or spiritual visions.

Ask your question now.

[Allow fifteen or twenty seconds to verbalize the question.]

Notice how the Spiritual Master responds to your words.

See how carefully he listens. See how thoughtfully he considers your question. Continue to observe the Spiritual Master closely.

The Spiritual Master may answer your question with a facial expression alone.

He may answer your question with a gesture of the hands or a shrug of the shoulders.

Or he may answer your question at some length with carefully selected words.

The Spiritual Master might even show you something. Some object or symbol might appear in his hands.

However the Spiritual Master answers your question, the reply will come at the count of three.

One . . . watch and observe carefully.
Two . . . the Master begins to respond.
Three . . . the answer is given *now*!

[Allow twenty to thirty seconds for the Spiritual Master's full answer to be received.]

What kind of reply did the Spiritual Master give you?
What answer did you receive?
How do you feel about what the Spiritual Master has conveyed to you? How do you feel toward the Master?
A student steps forward and indicates that you must leave now. The time allotted for your audience with the Spiritual master has passed.
Now, as you are saying goodbye, the Master reaches into his robe and brings forth a leather bag.
The Spiritual Master tells you that he has a very special gift for you. He wishes you to take the object with you.
The Spiritual Master opens the leather bag and hands you the special gift. Look at it.
See and understand exactly what it is.
Turn it over in your hands. Feel it. Smell it. Discover all you can about the gift.
At the count of three, its true significance will be revealed to you.
One . . . see and understand the meaning of this special gift.
Two . . . the meaning is becoming clearer.
Three . . . you *know* and *understand* the true significance of this special gift from the Spiritual Master.
Thank the Master, and tell him how you feel about him and his gift.
Say goodbye, for now you must leave.

*   *   *

As you walk down the path to the mountain trail, your thoughts are on the Spiritual Master, his answer to your question about your receiving visions and teaching dreams, and the special gift that he presented to you.

Once you are alone on the mountain trail, open your hand and look at your gift once again in the moonlight.

Is there anything that you overlooked when the Spiritual Master gave you the gift?

Understand even more clearly what deep significance this gift has for you.

Know that you have the ability to use this gift wisely and to its most positive advantage.

And now, with the thoughts of your visit to the Spiritual Master vivid in your mind, know and understand that you may return to his ashram whenever you wish once again to gain from his great wisdom.

At the count of five, you will return to full consciousness.

One . . . coming awake with the Spiritual Master's teachings firmly in your mind.

Two . . . coming more and more awake with the true value of the Spiritual Master's gift fully impressed in your awareness.

Three . . . more and more awake, feeling very good in mind, body, and spirit, understanding more completely how to receive dream teachings.

Four . . . more and more awake, feeling better than you felt in weeks and weeks.

Five . . . fully awake, filled with love, wisdom, and knowledge.

13

GUARDIAN SPIRITS NEVER GO OFF DUTY

Among the most dramatic accounts of the supernatural are those in which spirit beings intervene in the course of human events and accomplish the rescue of someone in peril, perform a miracle healing, resurrect the life of someone in the depths of depression and degradation, or cause a lost soul to rediscover the path to spiritual awareness. As you will see in this chapter of inspirational stories, it matters little if the entities involved in the accounts are called angels, Light Beings, spirit guides, or Elder Spirits, these benevolent guardians are never off duty.

An Angel Visitation Saved His Life

Bret Bradford enjoyed many happy times when he was a small boy. He remembers singing in the choir at Huffman Baptist Church in Birmingham, Alabama, and he vividly recalls his being "saved" and being baptized as a "very exciting time."

Then, in December 1972, when he was nine, tragedy struck the Bradford home. Bret's older brother Allen, who was eighteen, and their father, Charles, left one morning to go duck hunting on the Elk River near Decatur with two friends—and none of the four men ever returned.

For three long months, in spite of an extensive search on the part of the authorities, no trace of the men was found. Even their large Coast Guard–style boat had completely vanished.

At last, in March 1973, the four bodies were recovered by dragging the river. Bret's mother Jayne was convinced that foul play had been involved. She felt strongly that her husband's boat had been stolen, and Charles, Allen, and their two friends had been forced to attempt to swim to shore in the near-freezing water.

Terrible times were not over for Jayne and Bret.

In August 1973, before either of them had an opportunity to grieve properly or to recover from the effects of the loss of their beloved family members, Morris Coats, a distant relative who had appeared on the scene sometime during the search for Charles and Allen Bradford, kidnapped Bret and held him for $15,000 ransom.

Whatever possessed Coats to perpetrate such a cruel crime on his own kin can hardly be fathomed by normal men and women. Perhaps he figured that Jayne had collected a large sum of money from the insurance company and he somehow felt entitled to a share of it. Regardless of the warped machinations of his mind, the FBI soon caught up with Coats and his girlfriend, who had been holding ten-year-old Bret at gunpoint.

On August 11, 1973, *The Birmingham News* carried an account of the sordid act of family betrayal with a picture of the rescued boy, looking defiant in spite of a bloodied lip.

Bret freely admits that such dark events in his childhood had clouded his psyche and made him a troubled teenager by the time he entered high school in Birmingham. His older sister, who lived in Decatur, helped out by allowing Bret to finish high school in that city. Bret later returned to Birmingham to take some art and music classes at Jefferson State Community College.

We can now fast-forward to 1995.

At this time Bret lived in San Francisco, where for many years he had worked as a film processor in a photo lab. Active in Unity Church and a willing volunteer worker in church and community causes, Bret was on a meditation trip away from the city when his father's wedding ring, which he had been wearing since the funeral, fell off his finger.

Bret never found the ring, but he recognized that the act of losing it was truly symbolic.

At the time of his father's and older brother's deaths, nine-year-old Bret was told that he was now the man of the family and that he could not cry. Such a sentiment was reinforced through his childhood—even when he was kidnapped—and that had been a very heavy burden for a young boy to carry.

"Twenty-two years later, on the top of a grassy mountain in California, I finally released my anger and cried for my father and brother," Bret said.

Seeking Artistic Expression to Smother Awful Memories

About a year later, Bret was horrified to witness a fiery traffic accident just below his San Francisco apartment. He remembers watching as dozens of people gathered on the sidewalk below to stare at the flames consuming the truck that had turned over, exploded, and burned two people to death.

For days he was haunted by the graphic images of the nightmarish scene. And he couldn't get his thoughts off either the victims or those thrill seekers who had gathered to watch the twisted metal funeral pyre formed by the burning truck.

He enrolled in an art class and began making a plaster angel that he painted in goldleaf and mounted on stone base. Such artistic expression help to ease his mind.

A Doctor's Diagnosis Becomes a Death Sentence

In June 1996, Bret returned to Birmingham to visit his mother.

On July 12, he was sitting on the back porch, ruminating about death, when he suddenly felt the left side of his body go numb and icy cold. He was taken immediately to Carraway Methodist Medical Center, and the movement in the left side of his body began to return.

After a brief time of recovery, Bret concluded his visit to his mother and returned home to San Francisco. He hadn't been back long when the numbness began to return to his left side and he was forced to seek treatment from doctors. Their diagnosis, however, was extremely grim.

According to Bret:

> The doctors in San Francisco said that I had brain cancer and that I would not live longer than six months. I was scheduled to have a brain biopsy to confirm their diagnosis, but I refused. They told me that I was going to die and that there was no cure, so why let them go in and play with my brain? I figured that the neurosurgeon at the teaching hospital in San Francisco wanted to demonstrate brain surgery to doctors in training, and I decided that I didn't want to be a guinea pig.

Bret was also certain that the chemotherapy that had been prescribed was making him sicker. He had lost his appetite and his body was shriveling away.

"They transferred me to Davies Medical Center in San Francisco, where I began physical therapy in a ward for stroke patients," Bret said. "On August 2, I had another seizure, and I lost feeling on the right side of my body and I also lost some of my speech. I remember my physical therapy nurse looking at me with tears in her eyes, and I thought that was not a good sign. I thought for certain that I was dying. I started counting my blessings. I accepted my death and believed that my time on Earth was finished."

"Your Medicine Is Killing You!"

After he had accepted the grim medical facts that he was dying and that there was no hope of recovery,

Bret suddenly felt very peaceful and calm and he entered into a dreamlike or visionary state.

"I saw a woman I believed to be a patient advocate," Bret recalled. "She was very professionally dressed in a rose-colored outfit. She had reddish-colored hair, and the whole room around her seemed to be really rosy and pink. The light around her was like that of the early morning. It was bright, yet soft, with a pink cast to it.

"She asked me what I was doing taking the chemotherapy. 'That medicine is killing you,' she said."

When Bret awoke from his vision, he refused any more chemotherapy. Almost at once, his strength and appetite began to return. He gained weight, recovered movement in his arms and legs, and learned to walk again.

"The doctors decided that I must have suffered a stroke and didn't have brain cancer after all," he said.

In November 1996, Bret moved back to Birmingham, where he resumed creating his unique angel statues from aluminum foil covered with plaster.

Inside the figures he places herbs and stones representing the seven human chakras or energy centers. The angels are painted gold, silver, or bronze and mounted on a marble or granite base. Once an angel figure is completed, he anoints it with oil and takes it to Unity Church to be blessed. Everyone who receives or purchases one of the angel statues is placed on a prayer list.

The Return of the "Beautiful Lady"

When I spoke to him in July 1999, Bret, now thirty-seven, remarked that the day before had marked the third anniversary of his first seizure. All that remains of his ordeal is a slight tremor in his left hand.

"I can't play the piano as well as I could before my seizure and that's all right," Bret said. "This little tremor serves as a reminder of what could have happened to me."

The beautiful "lady" with the rose-colored aura who appeared to him in the hospital and told him to refuse additional chemotherapy has manifested to Bret on two more occasions. Once to fill him with peace and reassurance when a numbness occurred in his left hand and he was undergoing a MRI and a CAT scan. And on another occasion when he had an adverse reaction to medication.

"During that third visitation, my psyche appeared as though I was once again a ten-year-old boy, and she led me down a strange hallway with crystalline caverns off the path. I feel that these caverns represented the various ways in life that I could have followed. When I stood before the final cavern, I could see sparks of multicolored lights illuminating the darkness. I now know that angels can appear before us in whatever form we need to make us do what we need to do."

Helping Others Through Their Pain and Sorrow

Bret Bradford is convinced that his mission in life is now directed to helping others through their pain and their sorrow by sharing his own story of having survived one tragic incident after another.

"Three years ago I thought I was dying, and I accepted my fate," he said. "When I realized that I was not yet going anywhere, I promised the rest of my life in service to God.

"Whenever God presents me with the opportunity, I have begun to speak to groups and I've found that when a person is in the midst of a really dark moment, words of encouragement seldom penetrate through the wall of the negative experience. But if someone steps forward to share a time in his or her life when they thought the light would never shine again, but it did, I have seen miracles can happen."

Bret is convinced that when people hear real, true-life stories of the pain, sadness, and darkness that others have endured and how they eventually overcame their sorrows, they receive powerful inspiration.

"I know that I, too, received my greatest healings in a support group," he continued. "Just hearing others' stories gave me the strength and restored my hope that maybe I would pull through, too.

"I have found that when I share my story with others who feel as though their life has ended, they begin to feel that they, too, can make it. I am so grateful to God for allowing me to fulfill my purpose in life by sharing my story with others, and it is my prayer that people will find inspiration in learning of how the angels and God helped me to overcome my challenges in life."

Jayne Bradford told me that she had recently been awakened in the middle of the night and had got out of bed to see a bright light coming from under her son's bedroom door.

"It was as bright as a car's headlights," she said, describing the intensity of light. "The next morning,

Bret told me that an angel had visited him again during the night."

While some mothers might become overwhelmed by the thought of their son entertaining heavenly visitors, evidence of angelic presence manifests frequently in the Bradford home—and that is just fine with Jayne. "We get the most beautiful angel touchings and signs in our house," she said. "I have always loved angels."

And Bret will continue making his beautiful angel statues. "There's something joyous in me when I make them," he said. "Guardian angels are God's gift to us at the time of our birth. These holy angels escort us on our journey through life. They protect us, defend us, guide us, and minister to our needs."

A Mysterious Night Visitor Performs a Healing Miracle

Today, Beverly Hale Watson of Double Oak, Texas, is the highly respected author of eleven inspirational works, including such memorable titles as *Messages from the Dove, Keys to the Book of Revelation, Reflections of the Heart,* and *Death: Our Portal to Life.* In 1965, however, she was a frightened mother of two who sat in a bed in a private room on the Cancer Floor at Highland Park Hospital, anxiously awaiting a more complete evaluation of her medical condition. She had been told that the cysts and lumps the doctors had detected were very likely to be cancerous.

Perhaps many readers can identify with the stressful crisis situation faced by Beverly as she sat alone in her hospital room, trying her best to think only positive thoughts about the outcome of the surgery that had been scheduled for 8:00 A.M. the next morning.

At eleven o'clock that evening, she began working on a Sunday school lesson plan to divert her thoughts from the grim possibility that the doctors might detect cancer in her body. If that were so, if the surgery provided conclusive evidence that the lumps and cysts were malignant, she would be faced with the decision of how best to eradicate them.

She thought of her two small daughters and wondered if she would live to see them grow into adults with children of their own.

Mildly berating herself for considering a negative scenario, Beverly tried to focus on a more positive scene, one in which smiling doctors informed her that the cysts and lumps were benign.

As her mind tried sorting through the various courses of action that her life might take within the next few hours, she came to realize the absolute truth of the matter. She wasn't in charge of her life—God was.

Beverly remembers that precious memories started flowing through her mind in split-second intervals, followed by thoughts of things she still wanted to do. Realizing very well that she alone could do nothing to change her situation, she turned her head upward and said, "Let Thy will be done."

Then, in Beverly's own words:

"Instantly there appeared at the foot of the bed a Light Being, whose brilliance was like the sun. I felt tremendous love projecting toward me.

"At the same time, a surge of heat entered through the crown of my head, shot through my body, and exited my feet, leaving behind an inner peace that has never left me."

When the doctors operated on Beverly the next morning, they were completely surprised to find nothing. They were totally mystified by the change that had occurred in their patient since the last set of X rays had been taken.

Naturally, Beverly was ecstatic to hear the good news, and it was then that she knew for certain that a miracle had taken place the night before. She decided against telling her doctors about her "visitor," for fear they may have had her transferred to the psychiatric floor for evaluation.

Other Talents and Abilities Begin to Manifest

About three weeks after she was sent home from the hospital, Beverly noticed that she was beginning to *know* things that were going to happen to people. She also appeared to *know* things about certain people's pasts—and in each case, the individual about whom she derived this knowledge was someone who had come to her for help.

The more she responded to the information coming from her inner voice, the more messages she began to receive telepathically—until they seemed to be coming nonstop.

At that point, Beverly conveyed to the "Invisible Source" that she needed a better and more complete understanding of the mental transformation that was taking place within her. For the next twelve years, from 1965 to 1977, her mentors and teachers were both visible and invisible as she concentrated on achieving higher levels of spiritual enlightenment.

Learning to Identify Messengers of Light

Many years would pass before Beverly Hale Watson had another visit from a Light Being that manifested in completely visible form, but over the years she counted herself privileged to behold so many aspects of the "Kingdom of the Lord," including those who are of "His/Her flock which we know not." She acknowledges that she also learned the truth of the ancient warning: "Be careful what you ask for, because you just may get it!"

As she has journeyed down the path to spiritual enlightenment, Beverly has been aware of the Holy Spirit as her constant companion:

"It has presented itself in many forms," she explained. "I have heard its voice. It sounds masculine to me, and it definitely gets my attention. However, most of my information is received through thoughts, ideas, intuitions, dreams, and visions."

Beverly said that while she may not actually *see* her invisible Source, her physical body has become very sensitive to vibrational frequencies or energies that are around her. She can sense when her Cosmic Friends are nearby.

"Sometimes these Messengers of Light dress in feathers or fur and manifest as birds—especially hawks and crows—and cats and dogs," she said.

"Their messages are conveyed to me telepathically, and I am able to respond in like manner."

Beverly said that over the years she has had numerous contacts with angels, who have appeared to her as ordinary men, women, and children. "We've met in grocery stores, restaurants, on airplanes, at sacred sites, to name only a few places," she said. "Each of God's messengers just seemed to show up at the exact moment that I needed information, protection, or help."

At other times, Beverly said, the beings were invisible to her eye, but she could feel their presence: "Especially when I visited hospital patients, ministered to individuals in crisis situations, or felt the death of a loved one was imminent."

Since 1965 when she beheld the Light Being as she sat on her hospital bed, Beverly has known that we never walk alone during our time on Earth. "Heavenly representatives of the Light are always available to us, simply for the asking," she said.

Time to Move On to a New Assignment

Beverly considers her life as a series of adventures and assignments. She has worked at many different kinds of jobs, but it was during her tenure with the Salvation Army that she heard the quiet voice of the Holy Spirit whisper that it was time to move on to another assignment. Assuming her new adventure would be in the corporate world, Beverly gave her two weeks' notice and left her position with the Salvation Army.

On a Monday morning in 1987, as she started to get out of bed, she was quite astonished to hear Spirit's new plans for her: "From this day forward, My child, you shall work for Me full-time, writing My words."

Her first reaction to the new assignment was one of disbelief. But later that day, when she was working at her computer, a message came through to clear the screen.

"Beautiful thoughts permeated my consciousness. Words began to flow through me that I knew were not of my mind," she recalled. "I couldn't believe the speed at which my fingers could type without errors. I had started my new job for Spirit with an exhilarating experience!"

Beverly was told that her first book would be one of poetry and that each poem would deal with life situations.

"It would have an airbrushed cover in light blue, an embossed white dove, gold lettering, and five colors of ink," she said. "The title would be *Reflections of the Heart.* The person who would be responsible for the graphics and book layout would be Cynthia Seymour Hyder, a friend of mine, who had also worked with gifts of the Holy Spirit."

Since 1987, Beverly Hale Watson has been the vessel through which ten other books have been written. In addition, her inspired stories and messages have appeared in seventeen books by other authors.

In 1988, the Voice told her to form a nonprofit foundation to be called The Sevenfold Peace Foundation and that its bylaws and mission statement would be written by Spirit. The foundation's mission would be to publish and distribute books, provide a newsletter, and offer intuitive counseling, educational classes, and materials to individuals on their evolutionary path to spiritual awakening. In 1999, one of the foundations's major outreach programs has included establishing a prison library containing religious and spiritual books at a facility in Colorado.

Striving for Peace and Harmony in All Things

When people ask her to help them gain higher awareness and achieve a more complete expression of their true purpose in life, Beverly often hears Spirit reply, *Just be! You are love!*

At the same time, she understands that, unfortunately, most people do not understand that they are an expression of God in physical form and that they can reflect on an individual basis the Divine Essence that emanates from their hearts.

"You must walk your talk," she advises those who seek her counsel. "Actions speak louder than words.

"God resides in all people. When you are associating with others, try to seek the spark of Light or Divinity within them. You can love a person for who they are, but you do not have to love or approve of what they do.

"Remember, God is perfection, but it is we, through our personal choices, who find ourselves separated from the Creator Source. To everything there is a cause and effect. Monitor your responses and reactions to situations. Strive for peace and harmony in all things."

Beverly also reminds us that the greatest book we'll ever read is the *Book of Silence.*

"It is available to everyone who can stop the constant chatter of the mind," she said. "Within its pages one may discover the keys to Universal Truth, wisdom, knowledge, and understanding. It is in your meditative moments that the Voice within can be heard.

"People go to God with an assortment of prayers, requesting assistance, answers, guidance, miracles, and so forth. They do all the talking, failing to remember that they can't hear the answers to their problems if they don't take the time to listen.

"Ask your angel guide, your Messenger of Light, to provide you with information that will be for your highest good," she continued. "A few minutes of your time spent in silence can make the greatest difference in your reality. Messages will come to you in thoughts, ideas, intuitions, dreams, or visions."

Beverly Hale Watson's own work as a messenger of truth continues. She considers her assignment from Spirit to be an exciting, rewarding career that ceaselessly provides experiences beyond her wildest dreams, and she encourages other like-minded men and women to join her.

"Your soul knows why you are on Earth at this point in time," she said. "The answers to all your questions can be found simply by turning within. Follow your heartfelt feelings, act upon your thoughts and ideas, take notice when the subtle chills run down your spine or the hair on your arms stand on end. It is Spirit speaking to you."

An Elder Spirit Freed Her from the Slavery of Alcoholism

While we all wish to achieve the goal of self-mastery and to change our world to a place of happier existence, we may, on occasion, find ourselves so cut off from all contact with positive, supportive people that despair and depression gang up to sap our self-esteem seemingly beyond repair. It is in such situations that it seems that only a helping hand from a spirit guide can reach through the gloom and rescue lives that once appeared lost beyond all redemption.

It is difficult for me to believe that Sunny Chobeka-sepe [Medicine River], the woman I know as a dynamic sixty-eight-year-old Shawnee clan mother serving her People of the Red Tail, was once an alcoholic who teetered at the doorstep of an obscure and lonely death. It was as she was about to pass into the spirit world after a ten-day binge that her guide manifested to her and set her feet firmly back on a lifepath of spiritual service.

Enduring Many Years of Confusion and Abuse

At the age of ten, after having lived harmoniously with nature in an isolated wooded area surrounded by five lakes, Sunny was taken away from her tribal family and the Shawnee traditional way of life to attend the white man's school.

"After that," she said, "I was punished if I 'acted

like an Indian' or spoke my language. Because of
this, I did not do my vision quest at the usual age
of around twelve."

Sunny's life became "many years of confusion,
abuse, and survival." It wasn't until her children
were grown and she had endured years of alcoholism
that she had a spiritual experience that ended her
addiction and placed her feet on a spiritual path.

According to Sunny:

On January 23, 1984, after a ten-day binge
while I was isolated in a furnished room, a Female Elder Spirit appeared to me. I was alcoholic because I had zero tolerance for alcohol
and chemicals. I was literally at the point of
death. I had eaten nothing and had had little
water for ten days.

The image of the Elder Spirit communicated telepathically with her.

"I was given a choice," Sunny remembered. "To
walk on into death or to follow the purpose that I
had come to Earth to do. The choice I made is
obvious.

"There was only an apple in the house to eat, and
I remember crawling to the refrigerator to get it. As
I ate, sparkles of light like fireflies seemed to be all
around me before they entered my skin. My energy
slowly returned, and I was cured of my alcohol
addiction."

Disobedience Causes Spirit Contact to Withdraw from Her

Sunny said that Elder Spirit became a part of her. Her tastes in all things changed—colors, food, decorations, clothing.

"She stayed with me until 1992 when I was sixty-one and disobeyed a direct instruction by a spirit being who came to me as a deer," Sunny said. "At that time, all spirit contact withdrew from me."

The knowledge that her disobedience had caused the withdrawal of vital spirit contact so devastated Sunny that she began preparing for a vision quest.

A Vision Quest Brings About a Renewed Sense of Purpose

In October 1992, nine months after her unfortunate error in judgment, she spent four days and nights at Big Sur, California, crying for her purpose and asking how she might best help her people. She wanted to know how, in the years remaining to her on the Earth Mother, she could best serve to help accomplish the unity and harmony of American Indian peoples.

On the fourth day, having received no reply to her pleas, she was about to give up on receiving a significant vision. A number of minor spiritual manifestations had occurred around her, but nothing that responded adequately to her cry for an answer as to how she might best fulfill her mission in a meaningful way.

And then the white butterfly, who had been her

messenger all during the quest, bade her not to give up.

"Three crows came to sit on rocks in the Big Sur River just in front of me," Sunny said. "They looked straight at me, and I wondered what message they had for me.

"Then they all flew up together and showed me a red-tailed hawk that was circling a tiny rainbow in the sky. This tiny rainbow was similar to what is often called a 'sun dog,' but this time—and many more times to come—the rainbow appeared to me in no scientific relation to sun or rain."

The hawk circled the rainbow four times as Sunny watched in awe. "I *knew* this was the vision I had cried for," she declared. "As I watched, the tiny rainbow turned to rosy hue, which I could feel as one feels the rays of sunshine—not as heat, but as energy, a very powerful energy that filled me with overwhelming love."

Tears streamed down her face, and Sunny called aloud: "Are you my spirit guide?"

The rosy patch pulsed in answer.

Sunny called out, asking her purpose: "How can I help my people in the time that I have left on Earth?"

She knew then that her spirit guide and she were one in the energy. Every cell in Sunny's body was infused. She would soon receive a clear message as to her true mission on Earth.

Sunny Begins to Create the *Earthbridge Circle*

When she felt as though she was able to drive, Sunny left the Big Sur region, where she had gone on her vision quest.

In the days that followed, she was intuitively given the knowledge that she had received a new name, *Chobeka-sepe* (Medicine River), and that she was to create a newsletter for Native American prison inmates. Her mother had passed away to the Spirit World two years before and had left a small bequest to "help people any way you can." This seemed like the best use of her mother's wishes.

But while Sunny was a writer and had distributed a small family newsletter, she had no idea where to begin to fashion such a large undertaking. She had never given a thought to prison inmates in her life.

"All the necessary information came to me when I needed it," she said, "and six weeks later, in December 1992, our first newsletter went out to about 150 people all over the world. The name *Earthbridge* came to me in a flash of insight. Such insights are not entirely physical or mental, but both, and *certain* knowledge."

Since October 17, 1992, Sunny Chobeka-sepe's life has been consumed by the *Earthbridge Circle*.

"Over 500 prison inmates and supporters all over the world now call us their family," she said. "We have grown in numbers and in our love for one another. Many in prison found that there were people on the outside who cared, and those in the outside world found ways they could connect with brothers and sisters in the Iron Houses."

Sunny admitted that sometimes the work is "often discouraging, frustrating, and depressing—but it is as well joyous, loving, and gratifying." Her office wall is filled with the pictures of brothers and sisters, children and grandchildren.

"When one of us hurts, we all cry out," she said. "We have seen our relatives leave prison and struggle to stay on the Red Road in a hostile world. Some have grown with their family's love. A few have stumbled and gone back to prison. But all are always welcome in our family."

Each month, from about noon on the sixteenth until the morning of the eighteenth, she drops everything to fast and pray in silence, preferably somewhere outdoors on the Earth Mother.

"Many in the Circle join in the energy at this time," Sunny said. "I always know that I can go back to the source of energy and love by returning to the vision of the rosy glow of my spirit guide. When I am refilled with love-energy to overflowing, I must then give it out to all who wish to receive."

The *Earthbridge Circle* currently has nonnative supporters all around the planet.

"We welcome all who care for Earth Mother and Earth peoples," she said. "We now have friends in Belgium, France, Germany, Spain, the Netherlands, Norway, Italy, England, Ireland, Canada, Switzerland, Australia, and Japan. We work toward bringing back the spiritual and cultural ways of the American Indian. We are nonpolitical, but we struggle against any politics that will keep these ways from native people in prisons, reservations, or wherever else.

"We are the *Earthbridge Circle*, and we care. If your heart is sincere, you are welcome to join us."

14

BANISH NEGATIVITY AND BECOME A SPIRITUAL WARRIOR

Before you are ready to link up with the secret powers of the world of the supernatural and explore other dimensions of reality, you must accomplish the task of removing negativity from your life. In order to become an effective spiritual warrior and set out armed against the forces of evil and disruptive entities, you must come to know yourself completely, your strengths and your weaknesses, and strive to banish all negativity from your thoughts, words, and deeds. It is far better that you yourself discern the faults and failings of your spiritual armor and work to strengthen them before your darkside opponents locate them and use them to undermine your efforts to achieve higher awareness and God-realization.

Perhaps many of you share my failing of impatience. By becoming impatient and attempting to advance certain situations far too quickly, I sometimes bring about my own failure. By becoming impatient and dropping my guard to seize the moment, I have oftentimes opened myself to attack by disruptive entities.

Learning to be patient has been one of my most difficult challenges on my earthwalk. I see so clearly the images of my final goals that I want it all to happen *now*. I want to be able *immediately* to leap over all the physical, mental, emotional, and spiritual hurdles that impede the complete and final accomplishment of any task I undertake. I want to be able to look back in satisfaction that I have achieved a job well done.

Over and over again I read the holy books, which advise all earthly pilgrims that spiritual growth is a long process that requires steadfast patience and perseverance. And some of our wisest human minds have counseled patience as one of the higher virtues:

"He that can have patience can have what
he will."

—*Benjamin Franklin*

"Patient waiting is often the highest way of
doing God's Will."

—*Collier*

"Patience . . . is the soul of peace. Of all the
virtues, it is nearest kin to heaven. It
makes men look like gods."

—*Decker*

Perhaps it is because those of us who live more in the mind and in the spirit and in future tense have already *seen* the achievement of so many of our goals in our dreams and visions that we simply find it difficult to wait for linear time to catch up with the actual physical moment of material realization.

But we must learn to understand that while we abide in the material world, we are to appreciate the meaning of the words "in the fullness of time," and "for everything there is a season."

The Striving May Be as Important as the Goal

I am indebted to one of my spiritual mentors, Goethe, for granting me an understanding that has, in recent years, allowed me to temper my great impatience with my inability to achieve certain of my goals as quickly as I would like. One of the underlying themes of *Faust*, Goethe's great masterwork of world literature, is that the striving toward a goal may be as important—or even more important—than reaching the goal itself.

Of course, the goal of higher awareness is vital to your spiritual evolution, but you see, if you live always in the positive attitude of *striving* toward that goal, then, in one sense, you have already *achieved* your goal.

For example, to believe with all of your essence that it is better to give than to receive, to share rather than to hoard, is largely to have gained the goal of selflessness.

To live as though your life shall be transformed through your positive acts of striving to achieve awareness is already to have begun the transmutation from the clay of humanity to the cosmic cells of angelic intelligence.

It all comes down to a matter of attitude. The attitude of striving toward a goal of achieving higher awareness, of having made a total commitment to that purpose, has an enormously positive effect upon your lifestyle, upon your treatment of Earth's fellow creatures, and upon your ability to withstand the crises and despairs of living than will the final accomplishment of your purpose.

The achievement of your transformation as an evolved entity signals the accomplishment of your soul's spiritual evolution. But it will be your attitude of commitment toward such a goal that will make you a person worthy of transcendence into a higher being.

In Order to Link with the Positive Forces of the Supernatural, You Must Know Yourself Completely

An important step in the successful fulfillment of your desire to explore the world of the supernatural as a spiritual warrior is to spend some time in thoughtful examination of who you really are. It is only by knowing yourself as completely as possible that you will be able to enter into spiritual activities that will complement your strengths and seek to limit those encounters that will exploit your weaknesses.

"Know thyself," admonished the oracles of the Greeks, thus providing all humankind with one of the most useful pieces of advice ever uttered. The philosopher Diogenes stated that those words of self-examination were inscribed in letters of gold on the temple at Delphos and were regarded as divine.

"To reach perfection," Diogenes said, "we must be made sensible of our failings, either by the admonitions of friends, or the invectives of enemies."

Expressing a similar sentiment, Jeremy Taylor, a British clergyman, advised, "Observe thyself as thy greatest enemy would do, so thou shalt be thy greatest friend." And indeed, there will be entities from the darkside who will be observing your actions to determine your weaknesses.

The Roman Stoic philosopher Seneca suggested a daily period of self-examination: "We should every night call ourselves to account: What infirmity have I mastered today? What passions have I opposed? What temptations have I resisted? What virtues have I acquired? Our vices will disappear of themselves if they be brought every day to examination."

If you have a certain reluctance to engage in too much self-examination for fear that you might become discouraged with yourself and disappointed with your analysis of your strengths and weakness, Francis de Fenelon, a seventeenth-century archbishop of France, had an excellent answer to appease that inner dilemma: "Never let us be discouraged with ourselves. It is not when we are conscious of our faults that we are the more wicked: on the contrary, we are less so . . . Let us remember . . . that we never perceive our sins until we begin to cure them."

Goethe, the German scientist-author, spoke with candor when he said, "How shall we learn to know ourselves? By reflection? Never. But only through action. Strive to do thy duty; then shalt thou know what is in thee."

A Checklist Designed to Help You Prepare to Explore the Supernatural

To help you achieve that very special endeavor of knowing yourself, I have included a checklist that will permit you more completely to understand the Real You so that you will become more confident in exploring the world of the supernatural. The following questions are designed to enable you to perceive the true personality that you may often keep well hidden behind all the protective mental/emotional barricades that you have erected throughout the course of your earthwalk.

The most desirable use of the following queries for your self-examination would be to take the time to write down your answers or to speak your immediate responses into a tape recorder. If that does not seem appropriate at the present time, you can always come back to that task, one which I guarantee would prove to be extremely fruitful.

Whether you are prepared to write out your answers or if you wish to read the questions and take a few moments to consider carefully and thoughtfully your responses to each one, at this time begin to examine the checklist.

First, take a comfortably deep breath, hold it for the count of three, and then slowly exhale.

Repeat this process three times.

Sit in quiet reverie for a few moments, and then answer these questions as honestly as possible.

Understanding Personal Experiences

What are your earliest memories?
When you believe that you have recalled your very

earliest memory, allow your thoughts to explore deeper. Can you discover any memories that may have been buried or repressed?

Have you any memory of encountering your spirit guide or of meeting a spirit entity of any kind when you were a small child?

Take a moment to experience those far memories with your senses. What sounds, odors, touch sensations, tastes, and images are associated with them?

Holding the feelings from those memories in your mind, reflect upon what sensory details have been most vivid in your experience during the past few weeks.

Have you any memories of recent encounters with supernatural beings within the past few weeks?

Which of those details have you most enjoyed?

Which have bored you, disgusted you, or frightened you?

What place do you most remember because it is associated with former happy times?

What place do you most remember because it is associated with past sorrows or awful times?

Can you recall a school—perhaps a particular room in that school—that is closely connected with your early inspirational and intellectual development?

Can you remember a church or synagogue that is closely associated with pleasant or unpleasant memories in your childhood?

Do you remember some place or home clearly because you learned something significant while you were there?

In the homes that you have known best, was the prevailing atmosphere—positive or negative—due to the conscious or unconscious effort of one person or a group?

Did you ever sense an unseen presence in any of these homes?

Did you ever see a spirit entity of any kind in any of these homes?

Is there a place where you know that you would never want to live or to visit again?

What was your favorite childhood activity before you entered elementary school?

What was your favorite activity in high school or college?

What is your favorite activity at the present time in your life?

At the same stages—pre–elementary school, high school, or college—what did you most dislike to do?

What activity do you dislike most at the present?

What sports or physical activities have you enjoyed at some time in your life?

Have you basically preferred organized or unorganized physical activities?

Do you remember any tense or stressful moments centered around a physical activity or sport?

Can you recall any positive or thrilling moments centered around a physical activity or sport?

What physical labor have you tried—and enjoyed or disliked?

What is the most exacting skill or task that you have accomplished?

What do you consider to be the greatest personal problem with which you have ever had to deal?

What do you foresee as the greatest problem in your future?

What troubles and fears have you experienced at different stages of your past? Did you—or do you—

attribute any of these troubles and fears to the presence of seen or unseen spirit entities?

What have been your saddest experiences in life?

Did you sense supportive or disruptive entities around you during these experiences?

Understanding Your Personal Relationships

What person did you most admire in your childhood before you entered elementary school?

What person did you most admire in grade school . . . in high school . . . and in college?

What person do you most admire at the present time?

Throughout your past, with whom did you feel you got along better, your father or your mother?

With whom do you get along better today, your father or your mother?

How would you describe the kind of person with whom you would best get along?

Name the persons who have had a definite influence on you.

Did you ever meet someone who forced you to feel inferior?

What is your true basis for really liking someone?

What is your true basis for really disliking someone?

What kind of person amuses you?

What kind of person is bound to antagonize you?

What type of man or woman is certain to stir feelings of sympathy within you?

What sort of individual will be likely to arouse feelings of admiration within you?

What kind of person do you dislike for no good reason that you can explain?

What actual individual in your experience have you taken an instant dislike to with no sound reason?

How do you usually react to small annoyances or irritations?

Understanding Your Interaction with Groups

Have you ever experienced group disapproval?

Have you ever been made to feel ashamed before a group?

Have you ever been disappointed because you did something well and failed to receive group praise or approval?

Have you ever held an unpopular opinion or belief? What was the result of your taking such a stand?

Have you ever courted favor from someone in authority over you?

Have you ever broken the code of behavior accepted by your family, friends, associates, or community?

What were the results of your behavior?

Do you feel that you are able to understand people whose religious, moral, political, or social ideas differ from yours?

Understanding Your Innermost Concerns and Apprehensions

Have you known failure in spite of experiencing strong feelings of responsibility or duty?

Have you experienced awful fear? Was this fear the result of a seen or unseen person or presence?

Identify the things or situations that you fear the most.

Have you ever sought to find out something that was really none of your business?

Have you known a very painful moment of misunderstanding between yourself and a loved one or a close friend?

Have you been the victim of envy?

Do you truly seek to place your mind and your emotions in agreement with one another?

During moments of introspection, have you discovered an inferiority complex or any other defense mechanisms within yourself?

On which subjects are you aware that you will quite likely rationalize? When it is just you sitting here all alone, what opinions or beliefs do you hold that are probably irrational prejudices?

In crisis situations, do you most often rise to meet the challenges—or do you become helpless and frightened?

Are you afraid of being alone?

What is the loneliest moment that you have ever known?

Have you ever discovered an undesirable character trait in another person whom you valued and then lost confidence in that person?

Have you discovered any undesirable character traits in yourself?

Have you ever discovered racial prejudice or some other prejudice in yourself of which you had previously been unaware?

Do you have a physical deformity, or have you ever had an accident or been wounded in a way that made you feel conspicuous?

Are there irrational ways in which you fear other people?

Are there aspects of the supernatural for which you hold irrational fears?

As you analyze your formal educational background, what influences derived from this experience do you now believe to have been of the most value to you?

What educational influences do you consider now to have been detrimental to you?

What informal education has been most important in your life?

Understanding Your Innermost Thoughts, Beliefs, and Principles

What principles do you cherish so strongly that you would act on them spontaneously in the time of a crisis?

Have you ever had a serious confrontation with your parents, friends, or associates over your principles?

Do you feel that you have a sharply defined sense of authority?

Do you admire a strong sense of personal integrity in others or do you really prefer conformity in other people?

Have you experienced insecurity from external forces or circumstances, such as illness, death, drought, depression, disaster, or war?

What basic attitude toward religion or morals prevailed in your family structure when you were a child?

What are your real beliefs about organized religion today?

What is your personal definition of God?

What are your actual beliefs about survival after death?

What fears do you harbor concerning the rewards or punishments of the afterlife?

Have any of the above beliefs changed as you have grown older?

Are there any important issues on which you have not yet developed a personal philosophy?

Do you believe in cooperation or do you prefer unrestrained individualism?

Do you believe that happiness or love comes more readily from self-centeredness or from unselfishness?

Now that you are alone and need not recite the conventional and acceptable platitudes, what really makes you happy?

Have you developed a basic philosophy about your place in the community . . . the world . . . the universe?

Have you developed a basic philosophy about the equality or inequality of husband and wife?

Do you believe that you have some freedom in which to shape yourself and your own future, or do your really believe that it is only important that you *act* as though you had the freedom to shape your own destiny?

Do you reconize any forces—seen or unseen—that may impose limits upon you and your future?

What forces—seen or unseen—do you feel that you have the ability to use to shape your future?

During your personal evolution and growth, have you changed your attitude toward death . . . immortality . . . a formal religious belief?

Have you felt the transient quality of human life?

Do you experience satisfaction when you dare to

be yourself instead of following custom or convention?

What is your attitude toward the future?

Identify the specific fears and hopes that you have for the future.

Abolish Fear—Recognized or Repressed

Generally speaking, it is some fear, recognized or repressed, that causes us to be negative and thereby to make improper judgments. Worry, anxiety, tension, panic, frustration, and hostility are the results of negative thinking. Fear causes uncertainty, doubt, and timidity, preventing you from achieving what could have been yours through good judgment.

You have spent your entire life acquiring negative memories, so the time is long overdue to abolish them.

All of us suffer to some degree from such painful thoughts. Whether they are embarrassing or unpleasant, we remember them and tend to dwell upon them, viewing and reviewing them, tormenting ourselves with the way we *should* have handled a particular person or situation.

Unfortunately, this act of viewing and reviewing such painful moments reinforces the agonizing memory, frequently magnifying it until it becomes even more deeply carved into our psyches.

By the time that we reach adulthood, most of us have accumulated a mental storehouse full of the memories of all the battle scars of our lives. Some people make the common mistake of daily reviewing their psychic injuries, as well as their old emotional bruises, just before falling asleep. In doing so, they peel back scar tissue and reopen their wounds, which amplifies their suffering and feelings of negativity.

Those who are guilty of this form of self-sabotage cite various rationales for such negativity. Some say they review their past painful scenes so they will never again fall into such situations. Others claim that by comparing the former attitude that they feel brought forth such a wound, they can see how much they've grown. Still others contend that the more they review the old hurt, the less sting it carries for them.

Perhaps you are guilty of any one of all three of the above rationalizations. All are *negative*; all are self-destructive.

To become positive, you must replace the negative output cluttering your mind.

You must fill yourself with positive memories, positive images—images of moments when you achieved goals, received praise, and were highly successful in your accomplishments.

View and review those scenes of positive accomplishments until their memories are indelibly imprinted on your mind.

Replace the Negative with the Positive

Play this little game with yourself:

Whenever you have received a harsh comment or criticism from someone, feed your psyche some positive memories.

Let's take a really simple example. Let's say that

someone has just mocked your choice of wearing apparel.

Immediately recall a time when you were complimented on your particular choice of clothing.

View and review that moment.

Allow the memory-echo of that the former complimentary phrase to ring and ring in your inner ears. Soon, you will remember only the positive statement and ignore completely the negative comment.

This is one of the ways by which you may combat negative thinking, a negative self-image, right on the very spot where it occurred.

Reexamine Your Past Mistakes in a New Light

Another way of taking a giant step toward banishing negativity is to examine your past mistakes, your old embarrassments, in a new light.

Perhaps you may have been far too young to handle a responsibility given to you.

Perhaps anyone, unprepared, would have handled the situation similarly.

Give yourself the same break that you would give another person.

Be as understanding with yourself as you would be with others.

Dismiss the negative images for good. Think of them no more.

If they attempt to reenter your mind, gently wipe your mental blackboard clean of all negative impressions.

Gaining Strength and Awareness from Pain and Sorrow

Many times we are confused by our lessons born in sadness—yet they may have been the ones that brought us the most awarenesses.

Many of us have felt a painful experience, a judgment we have assessed as a bad one, to be negative. Later, we realize that we have misjudged the experience due to our limited vision.

We cannot always see the total picture—or the growth in awareness that we will receive from having experienced the painful event. Instead, we often bear the emotional pain, shut our eyes to the possible growth potential, and deem the experience negative.

Strive Always to See the Total Picture

It is likely that we all have at least one major event in our lives that we do not fully understand, that, perhaps, we feel was brought to us solely for an evil or negative purpose. If we could view all of our life pattern from an eternal, timeless realm, we would be able to perceive that most of our sorrows result from our inability to understand and to comprehend the total picture.

We can make great strides toward exercising good judgment in all situations if we learn to change our perspective on things. We actually grow by enduring and by seeing through to the end those experiences that superficially appear to be evil or negative.

With the passage of time, after emotions have cooled—or after gaining fuller awareness—we may

view events from a much clearer and different perspective. What at first might have been regarded as
a curse may now more clearly be perceived as a
blessing in disguise—a blessing that has permitted
us to gain greatly in awareness.

As long as we seek truth and proceed forward on
the path of our mission toward the Source, no evil
or negativity can truly befall us—and we become
more fully equipped to link up with the secret force
that emanates from the world of the supernatural.

Fighting Evil and Negativity
as a Spiritual Warrior

My friend Dr. Evelyn Paglini states that she knows
that her soul is on a divine quest to learn about the
universe and to become one with all things. She is
also very much aware that she is here on Earth to
serve as a spiritual warrior, fighting evil and negative forces.

Born into a centuries-old family of the Genessian
religion, practitioners of natural magic, Dr. Paglini,
who currently resides in Sherman Oaks, California,
is a very well-known teacher of the powers of magic
and meditation.

"I had a sense of purpose at a very early age," she
said. "As early as two years old, I was communicating with spiritual beings and entities."

Receiving a Centuries-Old Legacy

One day, when Evelyn was about three-and-a-half, her grandfather gathered the family's children around him to search for a successor to whom he might pass on the legacy of his knowledge and power. Since most of the practitioners in the Genessian religion are usually males, little Evelyn was overlooked by her grandfather until she approached him and began speaking in tongues.

"I told him that I was the one he was looking for," Dr. Paglini said, "and he soon realized that magic had existed in many of my past lives and that the knowledge that I possessed was true. By the age of four, I was initiated into the Genessian religion and the practice of magic."

A Precise Discipline and Regimen to Become a Spiritual Warrior

Dr. Paglini recalled that her grandfather and her father set up a very precise regimen to teach her the discipline, balance, and determination needed for the practice of magic.

"I was taught how to understand and to utilize nature and the elements," she said. "I was instructed how to control the mind through meditative techniques in order to manipulate energies that could affect the outcome of the subject being targeted.

"It was a time filled with joy and wonder as I was being shaped to fulfill my purpose of becoming a spiritual warrior and teacher."

Dr. Paglini said that for several years her grandfather worried that she would not have the dedication that it would take to become a spiritual warrior.

"But because of the influence of being born on the vernal equinox—the Alpha and Omega of the Zodiac—I had the joy, expectation, sense of adventure, and power that goes with Alpha (the beginning) when it is joined with the Omega (the ending), the wisdom of the ancients," she explained. "This combination gave me the balance to overcome the temptations of straying from my purpose."

After many years of intense training to develop her gifts and her skills, Dr. Paglini was able to fulfill her purpose as a spiritual warrior and a teacher with passion, dedication, and confidence.

In her words:

As a spiritual warrior, I treasure my abilities to fight the battle on behalf of innocent individuals who are being victimized by negative or evil forces.

I find comfort in knowing that I am able to protect the blameless and to remove evil influences from their lives.

I am pleased that I can guide negative spirit entities into the Light, thus ceasing the havoc and fear that they have caused.

As a teacher, I enjoy instructing people how to help themselves. When people get involved with nature and the elements through the practice of magic, they are going to see divine energy around them and in them.

When they learn how to manipulate energy and are able to achieve a positive outcome, they become empowered to better themselves, as well as their loved ones and, hopefully, all of humankind.

My purpose in life means everything to me. It has given me the opportunity to be in awe of the Creator and the freedom to realize my own person. It is an anchor that steadies me during life's challenges—and it has shown me that we are eternal.

In the next chapter we shall allow all those who deem themselves serious explorers of the supernatural world to link up with the powers of the "S-Force."

15

BECOME ONE WITH THE SUPERNATURAL FORCE THAT GOVERNS THE UNIVERSE

The Universe is governed by laws that never fail, by forces that work without the interaction of human consciousness. Many of these energies, these powers, go beyond the present understanding of our sciences and technologies, so we call them "supernatural."

Although we cannot yet explain these forces, humankind does have the psychic ability to tap into the energies governed by these universal laws. We have the ability to utilize the infinite current of this supernatural power, this "S-Force," and channel it into positive actions of prayer, mystical expression, healing, and contact with multidimensional intelligences.

Our Soul, the essential Self within each of us, has eternal awareness, eternal consciousness, eternal wisdom, and eternal existence. We have within us the ability to interact with a Supreme Consciousness more powerful than our own, whose boundaries are without limits, whose awareness comprises all of the Universe.

Throughout the ages, our most revered master teachers, prophets, and mystics have told us of the universal powers that are available to us through the supernatural force that permeates our entire planet. As they sought to better understand this force, to better define it, they have given it names such as *prana, mana, ki, chi, wodan,* the Holy Spirit, the *ruach ha-kodesh.*

Down through the centuries, whether spontaneously or through disciplined training, seers, shamans, and psychics have learned to control the S-Force. The Algonquins' *Manitou,* the Sufis' *Baraka,* Plato's *Nous,* and Aristotle's Formative Cause are all names, terms, and concepts which epitomize humankind's persistent attempts to identify and define the supernatural energy that the more sensitive of our species have always known existed around them.

In some way we have not yet fully defined, the human psyche serves as a conduit for this energy that, in turn, enables telepathy, psychokinesis, prophesy, clairvoyance, levitation, and so forth to be manifested. With access to this unknown energy, we can overcome all obstacles that may seek to interfere with the accomplishment of our attaining higher awareness and God-Realization. Each one of us can become a conduit through which this supernatural force flows. We can become quite literally divine supernatural instruments, capable of sending and receiving energy.

Komar Challenges Us to Channel the S-Force to Realize Our Potential

My friend Komar has been listed numerous times as a master of physical feats in the *Guinness Book of World Records,* and he is the holder of many world records in endurance and pain control. In addition to lying on beds of nails, surviving the press of great weights, and bending steel bars with his bare hands, Komar can demonstrate his control of the S-Force by walking on beds of red coals at temperatures as high as 1500 degrees F to the satisfaction of committees of medical doctors and scientists.

Since Komar and I have been close friends for more than thirty years, I am certain that he will not be offended when I stress the point that he is no massive behemoth of rippling muscles. He is of less than average height, of cheerful, but ordinary appearance, and he supports himself and his family by working in a cheese factory in Ohio.

Komar was activated through a series of dream-teachings when he was a child and has experienced contact with multidimensional beings as an adult. One day he simply *knew* that his psyche could serve as a conduit for an unknown, unnamed energy—the S-Force—and that he could quite literally accomplish any feat of strength or endurance that he wished. With childlike enthusiasm, he demonstrates his ability to control pain through altered states of consciousness and he takes great pleasure in teaching others how to go and do likewise.

Some years ago, when Dr. Norman Shealy was Director of the Pain Rehabilitation Center, St. Francis Hospital, La Crosse, Wisconsin, we asked this expert in human physiology to examine Komar thoroughly. Contained within Dr. Shealy's extensive report was the following analysis:

It is obvious that Komar has the ability to distract his mind by going into at least an alpha state of consciousness—and in it to have control over his autonomic nervous system. Komar uses this state of mind to prevent pain and body damage.

What Komar seeks to accomplish in his public demonstrations is a shock effect that will excite people into realizing that they live their entire existences without even beginning to utilize their full mental capacities. Komar is challenging everyone that if he can learn to use the S-Force, so can they. And they don't need to practice feats of strength and endurance. They can develop the power of prayer, the ability to heal themselves and others, the facility of communicating with spiritual beings, and the will to become more complete and fully functioning humans.

Consciousness and the S-Force

Those bold-thinking scientists who have begun attempts to isolate the S-Force had first to begin to apprehend consciousness as a nonphysical, but very real, quality. And they had to understand that physical reality is connected to consciousness by means of a single fundamental element—the S-Force, the unknown energy.

In this view, consciousness is more than a biochemical phenomenon confined to our physical bodies. Consciousness is also a force or energy that partakes of a nonphysical realm unbounded by the constraints of linear time and three-dimensional space.

If this is so, the act of mobilizing our consciousness becomes an act of psychic functioning that may impinge directly along the entire continuum of reality—from consciousness to energy to matter. Thus, anyone who is capable of directing consciousness with intense focus and concentration should, hypothetically, be capable of significant psychic functioning.

Seeking to Define the S-Force

Science long ago discovered that everything is vibration. Everything, regardless of how solid it may appear to the physical senses, is vibrating at its own particular frequency. Every human being, every animal, every band of metal sends out short waves of different lengths. What is more, these personal wavelengths are as individual as fingerprints.

It has further been discovered that within every living organism there exists an energy, which, however weak, however unpredictable, can be refracted, polarized, focused, and combined with other energies. Sometimes it seems as though this energy has effects similar to those of magnetism, electricity, heat, and luminous radiation—yet it truly appears to be none of these things.

As an intriguing paradox to the current analyses of science, it may be said that while the unknown supernatural energy is often observed in the operation of heat, light, electricity, magnetism, and chemical reactions, it is somehow different from all these known forces and energies. The S-Force appears to fill all of space, penetrating and permeating everything. Interestingly, denser materials seem to conduct it better and faster. Metal refracts it. Organic material absorbs it.

The S-Force is basically synergetic, which, simply stated, means that it is a very cooperative energy—one that blends well with other energies.

Therefore, it might be said that the S-Force has a basic negentropic effect, which makes it the opposite of entropy, the expected disintegration and disorganization of matter. Somehow, the S-Force manages to violate the Second Law of Thermodynamics. It has a formative and an organizing effect. Just as heat increases, so does the effect of the unknown energy.

At some level of the universe, the S-Force blends and interconnects each of us to the other—and to all living things. On some level of consciousness, every living cell is in communication with every other living cell.

In certain experiments seeking to photograph with highly sensitized film the S-Force around psychic sensitives, spirit mediums, shamans, and yogis, it was found that the life-giving synergistic energy is blue in color. The entropic, disintegrative energy, on the other hand, has been photographed as yellow-red. It has also been discovered that the synergistic energy projects a cool, pleasant feeling, while the entropic energy produces a feeling of heat and unpleasantness.

It would appear that all humans, animals, and plants contain within themselves a series of geometric points in which the energy of the S-Force may become highly concentrated. Such points seem to correspond to the seven zones of the human body identified in the ancient East Indian philosophy and practice of yoga.

These seven zones, according to yogic teachings, are governed by neurohormonal energy centers known as chakras. These seven chakra centers emanate from the spine, and when they are "open," operating at their fullest capacity, yogis believe they grant total control over the individual mental, physical, and spiritual selves.

Opening Your Seven Energy Centers to Direct the S-Force

Although there are, of course, many methods by which you may tap into and direct the universal energies and the S-Force, it may be useful to examine certain yogic exercises of opening the chakras as technique that might work very well for you.

The seven chakras begin with the base of the spine, the sex glands. The first of the energy centers controls the male and female generative organs of life and reproduction.

Keep in mind the polarity of all energies that exist on the physical plane. The negative expressions of the first energy center are anger, greed, and lust.

The second energy center is in the lower abdomen, and it controls your body's lower portion, specifically your legs and your hips.

For a moment, center your attention on this chakra in the lower abdomen. Close your eyes and feel the energy come into that area and emanate from it.

As you direct your attention toward this area, you should be able to feel a tingling vibration in your

legs. Focus for a moment on the energy that emanates from this chakra.

The third chakra is in the upper abdomen. This
center controls the upper abdominal region, thereby
affecting all abdominal functions. This center, like the
others, restores balance and harmony and cleanses
all that it governs.

Take a moment to direct your attention to this chakra and allow yourself to feel a slight tingling vibration in this area.

The fourth chakra is the midchest, your heart chakra. This particular center is blocked in many individuals, because their mental and spiritual awareness
will not permit them to experience universal, unconditional love.

To cause this center to operate at its fullest capacity
with balance and harmony, you must learn to practice a nonjudgmental love toward all living things.
Take a few moments to focus your attention on your
heart chakra.

If you are currently experiencing a disagreement
or a quarrel with another, visualize that person's face
before you and transmit loving thoughts toward him
or her. An imbalance in your heart chakra can cause
a number of ills and malfunctions. Concentrate on
projecting feelings of love toward all humanity and
all living things.

The fifth chakra is in the neck, and it controls and
balances the upper torso. It affects your communication. When this area is closed or imbalanced, you can
lose control of your physical self.

This chakra influences your arms and your throat, and it is sensitive to various pressures, currents of energies, temperature variations, and so forth. Balancing and opening this energy center permits you further control of many of the glands and organs of your physical body.

The sixth chakra is commonly know as the "third eye," or your individual consciousness. Close your physical eyes and permit the energy of the S-Force to pulsate into this region between your eyebrows.

Feel the energy of that which underlies all supernatural phenomena and which is an essential aspect of all life on this planet pulsating in the region between your eyebrows, your "third eye."

Fix your attention on this center of energy. Not only will you balance your physical body, but you will begin to contact your higher spiritual self.

Continued contact with your spiritual self will put you in touch with another, more important aspect of your being, your Soul, your inner eye of wisdom. Through contact with your inner eye of wisdom, you will learn detachment from the physical world and grow in greater harmony with the cosmos.

It is through the sixth chakra, your third eye, that you will learn to become One with the supreme consciousness that flows throughout the Universe and you will achieve control of the supernatural force that touches all life on earth. It is through the third eye that all that exists may be made known to you.

The seventh chakra, the crown chakra at the top of your head, is the master controller.

When you learn to open, govern, and balance this

chakra, the egocentricity that separates you from all of life will disappear. You will become one with the God Force, one with the supernatural force, one with the Source of all things. From this awareness, you will attain eternal life, peace, wisdom, knowledge, and superconsciousness.

It is this chakra that permits you full and complete contact with your Higher Self, your Soul. This state of ultimate Oneness with the Universe is known in east Indian philosophy as "Nirvana."

Now that you are aware of the energies available to you and know of the centers of your body through which the supernatural force can be channeled, you may take the next step to achieve mastery of your mind, body, and spirit and assume full control of your life and the safe and successful exploration of what is known as the world of the supernatural.

An Exercise in Balancing and Opening the Chakras to the S-Force

Before you begin this exercise, be certain that all of your bodily needs have been acknowledged. You should be wearing loose, comfortable clothing.

Place your body in a comfortable position that you can easily maintain for at least a half an hour.

If you have the ability to assume the lotus position, do so. If this would be uncomfortable for you, sit straight-legged on a cushion with your back to the wall or lie down on a cushion or blanket.

Soft background music could be a very effective aid to this exercise. You may also wish to have some-

one read this technique to you or make a tape of this
method in your own voice.

The Process

With your eyes closed, begin breathing in comfortably deep breaths.

After a minute or so, begin to breathe more slowly,
in deep measured breaths.

Breathe in this manner for two or three minutes,
clearing negative thoughts and concerns from your
consciousness.

Become sensitive to the coolness of the air that enters your nostrils and the warmth of the air that
leaves.

Concentrate on this sensation for at least one
minute.

Continuing to take comfortably deep breaths, feel
your body consciousness beginning to leave the
lower, material existence for the higher levels of
consciousness.

Feel yourself leaving the darkness for the light.

Feel yourself leaving physical restrictions and rising higher to touch the eternal.

Feel yourself leaving the unreal world for the
true reality.

*Repeat the following suggestions mentally and feel the
resulting sensations move throughout your body:*

I am relaxing my entire body. I am relaxing my
feet . . . my legs . . . my torso . . . arms . . . neck . . .
face . . . my head.

My entire body is relaxing . . . becoming more and
more relaxed.

My breathing is getting deeper now . . . slower now . . . deeper now . . . slower now.

I am completely relaxed.

I am now aware of the energy of the supernatural force that surrounds me. I can feel this energy around me. I know that this is the same supernatural force that governs the blessed harmony of the Universe.

My entire body is bathed in the supernatural force that is a part of all life on this planet.

My entire mind is bathed in the energy of the supernatural force.

With every beat of my heart, the energy of the supernatural force pulsates within me.

I can feel the energy pulsating all around me, throbbing together with my own individual life flow.

With a deep breath I draw this energy into me, into my body, into my mind, into my spirit.

I feel the energy nurturing me, nourishing every cell of my body, filling me completely. Each breath that I take draws more of the energy of the S-Force into me.

My mind is gathering this energy and focusing it at the very base of my spine. I feel the energy collecting at the base of my spine, humming, tingling, vibrating, and opening my first chakra.

I feel my first chakra opening, and I feel very positive and very blessed.

The energy of the S-Force travels up my spine and bursts into my second chakra, my abdominal chakra.

I can now feel my abdomen and my legs becoming balanced and in harmony with all that is positive.

Now the power of the S-Force is traveling up into my upper abdomen, my stomach region, and I can feel my third chakra opening.

I feel balance, harmony, and health fill my being as my third chakra opens and becomes energized.

The supernatural force is now moving farther up my spine to my fourth chakra, entering the very heart of my nervous system.

I can feel my heart chakra opening wider, becoming balanced. I feel love, unconditional love, for all living beings, for all of life, for God, for the Universe.

My fourth chakra opens wide, and I feel the energy of the supernatural force enveloping me, warming me, and I am filled with love as I have never experienced it—a deep, warm, complete universal love.

Now the energy of the S-Force moves farther up my spine to my fifth energy center in my throat region. I can feel the energy entering now, opening now.

The energy is filling my being, and I feel it humming, vibrating, pulsating throughout my entire body.

It is balancing many of my glandular functions.

It is balancing all of me more completely. My fifth energy center is open.

Now the energy of the S-Force rushes into the area between my brows, my third eye, my sixth chakra.

I can feel the energy pulsating, tingling, throbbing. The energy feels so wonderful.

I now see a light before me.

The light is getting larger and larger. It grows larger and larger—until it covers the entire vision of my third eye. This is the light of the Holy Spirit, the *mana*, the *ruach ha-kodesh*, the *chi*, the *Baraka*.

I am now aware of my spirit, my Soul, and I feel it moving within me. It is becoming freer, more detached from the physical body.

I feel my Soul leaving the physical, lesser, reality for the truer, spiritual, all-encompassing reality.

I feel one with All That Is . . . one with the Universe. I can now reach the higher consciousness that governs the entire cosmos. I desire to know all, for I seek the Source of All That Is.

The energy of the supernatural force that governs the Universe is now blossoming forth in my brain, like a thousand-petal lotus blossom—opening up, petal by petal, one petal after the other.

I feel the life-giving, sustaining Oneness of the S-Force filling my mind completely, totally, fully.

I am in complete and total balance.

My entire mind, body, spirit is in balance, in harmony with All That Is and the Universe.

I am reaching for my higher self, my higher consciousness, my personal superconsciousness, my Soul.

I can feel all these energies entering my being together with the supernatural force. I merge into them. My Soul merges into me. We are one. All is one.

I now have the ability to use the S-Force as a power for good and for God and to explore other dimensions of Time and Space.

From this day forth, I vow to reflect my higher self, my Soul, in all that I do. As I am merged into my Soul and it is one with me, all things known to it are available to me.

I am one with my higher self in the timeless realm. All love and wisdom can now flow through my being with the supernatural force, and I know I shall be fulfilled in achieving complete knowledge of my true purpose in life.

16

MAINTAINING A MYSTICAL STATE OF CONSCIOUSNESS

We have presented many facets of the supernatural world in this book. Some provoked fear and apprehension; others inspired new insights and revelation. All produced life-altering changes in those who experienced a journey into the supernatural.

We have seen how ordinary, rational humans have responded to encounters with ghosts, angels, and entities from UFOs. Some of these mysterious beings—both seen and unseen—have brought with them miraculous healings, a new kind of musical expression, and inspiration to rise above all physical impediments and challenges.

We have met men and women who have undergone near-death experiences, witnessed the material appearance of spirit guides, and listened to compelling voices from other dimensions.

And consistently, we have also seen that a mystical state of consciousness is very often an integral element in the acceptance of the manifestation of entities and phenomena from the world of the supernatural—and such state of consciousness is surely a prerequisite in attempting to channel the S-Force.

William James's Four Criteria Defining a Mystical Consciousness

In his classic *Varieties of Religious Experience*, William James proposed four criteria that may differentiate a mystical state of consciousness from other states of consciousness:

1. *Ineffability.* The handiest of the marks by which I classify a state of mind as mystical [is that] it defies expression, that no adequate report of its contents can be given in words. . . . Its quality must be directly experienced; it cannot be imparted or transferred to others.

In this peculiarity, mystical states are more like states of feeling than states of intellect. . . . Lacking the heart or ear, we cannot interpret the musician or the lover justly, and are even likely to consider him weak-minded or absurd. The mystic finds that most of us according to his experiences are equally incompetent.

2. *Noetic quality.* Although so similar to states of feeling, mystical states seem to those who experience them to be also states of knowledge. They are states of insight into depths of truth unplumbed by the discursive intellect. They are illuminations, revelations, full of significance and importance . . . and as a rule they carry with them a curious sense of authority. . . .

3. *Transiency.* Mystical states cannot be sustained for long. . . . Often, when faded, their quality can but imperfectly be reproduced in memory; but when they recur it is recognized; and from one recurrence to another it is susceptible of continuous development in what is felt as inner richness and importance.

4. *Passivity.* When [mystical consciousness] has set in, the mystic feels as if his own will were in abeyance, and indeed sometimes as if he were grasped and held by a superior power. This . . . connects mystical states with certain definite phenomena of secondary or alternative personality, such as prophetic speech, automatic writing, or the mediumistic state. . . . Mystical states . . . are never merely interruptive. Some memory of their content always remains, and a profound sense of their importance.

Psychism, Creativity, and the Supernatural

I have often noted strong links between what one would term the psychic-sensitive, the mystic, and the creative personality. Many researchers have sought to develop some kind of pattern profile of the emotional, mental, psychic, and physical influences (and/ or stresses) that produce creative expression in certain individuals, and I think it not far off course to suggest that a combination of similar elements in one person may generate an artist, a musician, or a poet and in a slightly different person may produce a mystic, psychic, or a priest. There is very often that fine balance—that cosmic moment of choice, that delicate fashioning of opportunities lost into more advantageous opportunities claimed—that can decide which path one takes to fulfill his or her destiny.

The prophet, the mystic, and the psychic-sensitive appear to possess supernatural talents beyond the grasp of the average man or woman. But then, so does the accomplished artist, poet, or musician.

If one's talent with paints and canvas has never progressed beyond kindergarten finger painting, if one's dexterity on the piano keys has never surpassed "Peter, Peter, Pumpkin-eater," if one's gift for prosody has never eclipsed "Roses are red, violets are blue," then how extraordinary—how *supernatural*—must seem a talented artist, a piano virtuoso, or a compelling writer or poet.

Creativity must find an outlet, and whether it be in composition or in clairvoyance may only be some unique combination of circumstances and environment.

An Adventure in Consciousness That Led to Enlightenment

In his new book, *Toward Homo Noeticus: Reflections on God-Realization and Higher Human Development,* John W. White, author of such highly respected works as *What Is Meditation?* and *What is Enlightenment?* tells us that his present state of consciousness is the condition traditionally described in yogic terminology as *sahaja samadhi,* "easy enlightenment" or "open eyes enlightenment."

That is to say, he walks around and functions in everyday life rather than remaining absorbed and isolated in deep meditation.

"Quite simply," John said, "I see God in all things and all things in God. Hence I am one with the 'Father' and there is no sense of separation from God in any aspect of my existence. I am unconditionally happy."

Explaining that he does not seek to make grandiose claims about himself and hastening to state that he doesn't consider himself to be anyone special, White said, "Enlightenment highlights the similarities rather than the differences among people; it shows the enlightened person that he or she is, at rock bottom reality, just like everyone else—i.e., ultimately, we are all one."

Today John W. White's "career" is to communicate about enlightenment "and to let the Tao/Divine Will lead me."

"I regard myself as a self-consecrated man of God whose parish is the entire planet," White said.

"I've taken the bodhisattva vows and am trying to conduct myself as a *Rambodhisattva*, a peace warrior capable of dealing wisely and compassionately with the increasing violence and insanity of the world as humanity at large moves into the evolutionary stage of full-functioning ego, in accordance with the divine template for our destiny."

As White explained:

. . . I am embarked on an adventure in consciousness, exploring the human potential for apotheosis. Although I rest in the fullness of Being, I am nevertheless restless in the potential of Becoming. Like all people, I am both a human being and a human becoming.

Mystical Consciousness Provides a Focused Existence

Robert Brown, a writer from Marysville, Washington, said an "older voice" came to him at age five and informed him that he had a special mission in life.

"When I was young," he explained, "this 'voice' was an older version of myself. Now it is much like a loving twin, separate and unique, with the ability to cleave through any thought or conversation.

"As with any caring individual, the volume and content of the voice are regulated by the current moment, emotion, and event. The role of the voice in my life has been that of coach and mentor, here to guide my life, not live it for me."

The knowledge communicated to him by his "voice" has brought Robert great joy and internal peace.

"It allowed me to work through the recent passing of my father and uncle," he said, "and it has enabled me to help other family members who are grieving through the retelling of their stories of love. I literally feel driven to put down on paper all things of goodness, the acts of love, and the marvelous words of my guardian spirit.

"This focus on my mission drives away despair, shortens sorrow, and serves to place all events in an acceptable manner. The voice which initially set me on the right track as a child has pushed and prodded me throughout life in a nurturing way."

"Live Moment to Moment in an Attitude of Discovery"

In his novel, *The Paths of Awakening*, Robert Brown has "Michael," his protagonist, discussing life's purpose with his guardian angel. As he admitted to me, the angel's response is based on what he has learned from his own guardian spirit.

According to the spirit Michael:

More than anything, you are on a journey of discovery of who you are and what you have the potential of becoming. On a daily basis and often as close as moment to moment, these paths are presented to you.

If you would ask for a gift, ask for clarity of vision, for the gift of recognition of the wisdom that accompanies each little event. These thinly veiled truths meld with spirit and form your opportunities for growth and personal triumph. It is how you acknowledge and celebrate their arrival that is seen as the calligraphy of spirit and is recorded in the foundation of your character.

. . . [To live] moment to moment in an attitude of discovery and celebration . . . is a joy and gift that requires no witness other than itself.

The Joy of Becoming a Cocreator with God

As Robert Brown so aptly phrased it, a mission formulated by your mystical state of consciousness provides you with a purposeful, focused existence. In addition to the satisfaction of knowing that you have a purpose in life and that you are steadily moving forward toward the completion of your earthly mission, there is the great joy to be celebrated in the realization that you have become a cocreator with God.

As you direct the energy of the Holy Spirit, the *ruach ha-kodesh*, the Great Mystery, the S-Force through the conduit of your psyche, you will discover that you have the power to create your own miracles of accomplishment and spiritual attainment.

Prayer Can Set the Supernatural Force in Motion

In his *Religious Perplexities*, Dr. L. P. Jacks also speaks of this unknown energy or power and suggests that prayer may set in motion a force that answers the entreaties of each individual supplicant.

Dr. Jacks hastens to add that such power need not diminish the Divine:

> All the evidence of the religious experience shows us that man makes contact with this Power, which appears partly transcendent and felt as the numinous beyond the self, and partly immanent within him. I also think it likely . . . that it may well be this uplifting Power which does it fact activate the subconscious solution-providing mechanism in way which would not otherwise be possible. . . .
>
> In its essence the Gospel is a call to make the same experiment, the experiment of comrade-

ship, the experiment of fellowship, the experiment of trusting the heart of things, throwing self-care to the winds, in the sure and certain faith that you will not be deserted, forsaken, or betrayed, and that your ultimate interests are perfectly secure in the hands of the Great Companion. . . .

The Universe Is in a Constant State of Creation

In *The Seth Material*, Jane Roberts and her husband Robert Butts record the multidimensional being "Seth" explaining how the universe is in a state of constant creation and how humans become cocreators with God by utilizing the force within:

. . . God is the sum of all consciousness, and yet the whole is more than the sum of Its parts. God is more than the sum of all personalities, and yet all personalities are what He is.

There is within you a force that knew how to grow you from a fetus to a grown adult. This force is part of the innate knowledge within all consciousness, and it is a part of the God within you. The responsibility for your life and your world is indeed yours. . . . You form your own dreams, and you form your own physical reality. The world is what you are. . . .

. . . There is a portion of All That Is directed and focused within each individual, residing within each consciousness. Each consciousness is, therefore, cherished and individually protected. This portion of all consciousness is individualized within you.

Becoming Transformed by Love

My wife, Sherry Hansen Steiger, an ordained Protestant minister, lecturer, and author of *The Power of Prayer to Heal and Transform Your Life*, has observed that all products of human creation began as invisible thoughts in someone's mind.

"Those unseen thoughts reflected the pattern of their creator, just as we are the reflection of our Creator," she said. "Holy scriptures teach us that we were created in the image and likeness of God. That image is love and light.

"If we were to reflect our true nature, we would reflect a pattern of the life that is us—God. We would be One with the strongest force in the universe as cocreators with God. Then all that we created would be in perfect harmony and balance."

Sherry added:

As cocreators, we are not *the* omniscient-omnipresent God, but *aspects* of God. As a thread to a fabric or a teaspoon of water to the ocean, each and every one of us is an important and integral element in the universe.

As I wrote in my book *Seasons of the Soul*, each of us has within us the essence of God. As cocreators with God, we have the choice to remember who we are and always choose love over anger. And every time that we do, it is a miracle gathering momentum, gaining power.

Continue to choose love, and you will be allowing the real you to shine forth.

You were formed by love. Be *transformed* by love, and you will be the cocreator you were meant to be.

Minute by minute and second by second, as we allow ourselves to explore the unknown, we realize our destiny, our true purpose in life.

Developing a Greater Patience for the Foibles of the Physical World

Yet another benefit that accrues with a state of mystical consciousness is the enrichment of the higher characteristics and qualities in your life. You will enjoy a deeper sense of peace as a result of your communication with spirit, and you will achieve a great sense of wholeness, of oneness with all living things.

At the same time that you are developing a greater patience and tolerance for the foibles of the world, you will also begin to exhibit a greater and more robust experience of physical health.

Even if you have previously suffered a physical handicap or disability, the power of positive thinking that arrives as a benefit of developing a state of mystical consciousness is going to make you feel better.

Even if you previously came to accept a certain portion of pain as your daily human condition, your new attitude and your new resolution to become one with the supernatural force that governs the harmony of the Universe will enable you to rise above physical restraints to attain all your worthwhile goals.

Each new day will find you acknowledging that there is nothing that you and God cannot achieve together.

Seek Your True Supernatural Powers and Abilities

Throughout the text I provided a number of spiritual exercises designed to stimulate your awareness of the many facets of the supernatural world that surround us, and many of the men and women whose stories were included in the book were also generous in sharing their own special exercises, prayers, meditations, and spiritual techniques. It is my earnest prayer that you will be so moved by the inspirational stories in this book that you will resolve at once to seek out your true powers and abilities and strive to achieve higher awareness.

Examine All Philosophies Before Making Them Your Own Truth

By the same token, I want you to test each one of the concepts, experiences, and philosophies expressed in this book for yourself. In the silence and safety of your own sacred space, carefully evaluate the lessons presented for your study and assessment and make a conscious, prayerful decision whether or not they are also your truth.

In *The Dhammapada*, Gautama Buddha gives timelessly valuable advice to every sincere explorer of the supernatural world:

> Believe nothing, O monks, merely because you have been told it . . . or because it is traditional or because you yourselves have imagined it. Do not believe what your teacher tells you out of respect for the teacher. But whatsoever, after due examination and analysis, you find to be conducive to the good, the benefit the welfare of all beings—that doctrine believe and cling to, and take it as your guide.

Cautiously, Prayerfully Discern the Boundaries of the Supernatural

"What is man?" the psalmist asked, and concluded that to be human was to be but a little lower than the divine.

Modern materialistic science has reassessed the ancient, plaintive query and concluded that to be human is to be no more than an arrangement of biochemical compounds, a cousin of the laboratory guinea pig rather than a daughter or a son of God. Science, which has so wonderfully alleviated so many of the curses of the human condition, has levied a terrible blight in return if its mechanistic magic deceives us into believing that we truly are trapped in the same cycle that imprisons the atoms of hydrogen and oxygen.

By tapping into the as-yet undefined powers of the so-called supernatural through the S-Force, we may expand the material definitions of what is to be human and begin to reclaim our true cosmic heritage as sons and daughters of the blessed harmony that governs the universe.

As has been stated many times in this book, go into the Silence, seek the God within, and pray for the ability to discern the unseen spiritual boundaries of the supernatural that surround every inch of our world of material reality.

If you seek true knowledge and wisdom—or if you wish to intensify the awareness that you already possess—set about the task of purifying and ordering your life in the physical, mental, and emotional dimensions so that you may make yourself as perfect an instrument as you can for the Holy Spirit, the Great Mystery, the supernatural force that permeates every aspect of your earthly existence.

Although I have urged you to seek higher states of consciousness and to blend with Spirit, it is important that you do not set up preconditions as to how any gifts of awareness should manifest. When you seek a message or a new understanding, be careful not to allow your conscious self with its hopes and/ or fears to get in the way of a true revelation.

The exercises in this book were offered as methods whereby the proper mental and spiritual attitude of receptivity might be encouraged. If you have aspired to the highest level of spiritual consciousness, then it is my earnest prayer that you shall receive new understandings concerning your true purpose in life and be granted meaningful revelations.

When you are truly proceeding steadfastly forward on your exploration of the supernatural, you will find yourself becoming a true cocreator with God. You will find yourself more and more experiencing the Light, letting it flow through you, giving it force so that others may feel a portion of it through you.

As you practice the power of prayer and the unfoldment of meditation, you will find yourself wanting more and more to help others become more fully aware of the God within.

As you become one with the energy of the spiritual principle and with the universe, you will discover that ego has been absorbed into unconditional love for all things.

As you give up your earthly physical concerns for the attainment of spiritual balance, you will remember what you have always known—that you are an individual expression of God on an odyssey across time and space, a pilgrim soul on its mission of love and light.

References and Resources

Chapter Two: "Living with the Many Ghosts of Inspiration House"

Rita Gallagher remains active as a popular author of romance novels and as a respected teacher of writing workshops. She may be contacted by writing to her at PO Box 73686/Houston, TX 77273.

Chapter Three: "Lucy Fritch, The Friendly Spirit"

All the names in this account—with the exception of the ghost's, Lucy Fritch—have been changed at the request of the witnesses to the multifaceted phenomena in the old Southern mansion.

Chapter Four: "Bringing Peace to a House of Violent Death"

Names and places have been altered and the true identity of the hosts of the haunting have been changed to protect their anonymity.

257

Chapter Six: "The Other Face in the Mirror"

Names have been changed to guard the teenagers' privacy.

Chapter Seven: "Angels, Spirit Guides, Light Beings, and Space Brothers"

Information about Leslie Smith's proposed "Angel Directory" and other projects may be obtained by writing to her at PO Box 93393/Pasadena, CA 91109 or by visiting her Web site, www.angeldirectory.com

Lori Jean Flory may be contacted by writing to her at PO Box 1328/Conifer, CO 80433. Her E-mail is angelheart@bewellnet.com.

Brenda Montgomery may be contacted by writing to 2675 Hemlock/Morro Bay, CA 93442.

Chapter Nine: "A Ragged Stranger Reset His Moral Compass"

Information about Timothy Guy's book *Aliens Over America* may be obtained from AOA Press/PO Box 572377/Tarzana, CA 91357. 1-800-700-4024.

Chapter Ten: "The Seeress Who Talks to Spirits"

Clarisa Bernhardt may be contacted by E-mail at clarisabernhardt@hotmail.com or by writing to PO Box 669 Station Main/Winnipeg, Manitoba, Canada R3C 2K3.

Chapter Eleven: "He Collaborated with an Interdimensional Being and Became a Pioneer of New Age Music"

Iasos's Inter-Dimensional Music may be obtained in any record or music store or write to Iasos, 33

Varda Landing, Sausalito, CA 94965. His Web site is
www.iasos.com; E-mail: iasos@nbn.com.

Chapter Thirteen: "Guardian Spirits Never Go Off Duty"

Information regarding Bret Bradford's angel art
may be obtained by writing to New World Vision,
Angel Maker, 917 Stark Street, Birmingham, AL
35235 or contact his Web site, www.anewworld-
vision.com.

If you wish to learn more about Beverly Hale Watson's Sevenfold Peace Foundation, write to 215 Lake
Trail Drive, Double Oak, TX 75077.

For information about The People of the Red Tail
and the work of Earthbridge Inc, the vision of Sunny
Chobeka-sepe, write to PO Box 5786/Marianna, FL
32447.

Chapter Fourteen: "Banish Negativity and Become a Spiritual Warrior"

Dr. Evelyn Paglini may be contacted in writing at
14713 McCormick Street, Sherman Oaks, CA 91411
or by visiting her Web site, www.mysticalblend. com

Special thanks for their cooperation and the shar-
ing of their stories go to Kathleen Curry, Bridget
Martin, Freddie O'Malley, Bob Brown, and John W.
White.

The Steiger Questionnaire may be obtained by writing to Timewalker/PO Box 434/Forest City, IA 50436 or by visiting the Steigers' Web site, www.bradandsherry.com.